MERCHANT SHIPS OF WORLD WAR II

A Post War Album

VICTOR YOUNG

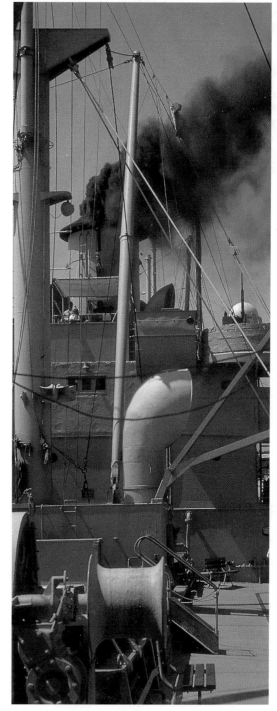

SHIPPING BOOKS

First published 1996 by Shipping Books Press
P O Box 30, Market Drayton, Shropshire TF9 3ZZ, England

British Library Cataloguing in Publication Data
A catalogue record for this book is available form the British Library.

ISBN: 1 900867 01 X

Cover Photographs
Front cover top   **Gloucester**, built 1941, arriving at Wellington, New Zealand in November 1965 (*see page 16*).
Front cover bottom   **American Produce**r, a 1943 built C2 type photographed in 1963.
Back cover   "Going Home" ... The war-built Empire tugs **Taioma** and **Tapuhi** steam across Wellington harbour in 1970. Hot coffee was on the galley stove. Deck boys talked of their social achievements on Friday night. The master studied "the orders" for Sunday.

Designed by Victor Young and Linda Machin
Typeset by MJP, Doveridge, Derbyshire
Printed and bound in the United Kingdom by Amadeus Press, Huddersfield

Introduction

Merchant ships built during the years of World War II. Some were conceived in peace, others came into being through the most urgent wartime necessity. While craftsmen shipbuilders created warbuilt ships in established shipyards, others came from the hands of farmers, shop assistants, labourers and housewives in shipyards as new as the ships themselves. Many ships were sunk, most survived, helping to rebuild the peace in a post war world. ·

There is now a generation of shiplovers for whom the World War II standard types are, at best, a distant memory. For those of us who knew and loved these ships, this is an album to revive memories. For the new generation it may serve as a window on a past era. Perhaps a small time capsule recording the passing of a type of ship, and a style of seafaring that has gone for ever.

In the 1950s and '60s colour photography was not as easily accessible, or of the quality, that we now take for granted. The result is that today, many who are interested in the ships of yesterday, have only a black and white image for reference. Most of the ships featured here are shown in the last stages of their commercial lives. Many went to shipbreakers a short time after the photographs were taken. This work is not intended as an in depth reference to World War II standard ships. There are many Allied and Axis designs not included. I have tried to illustrate a selection of survivors from the wartime standard fleets, as seen in the world's ports twenty or more years back. Ship types are grouped together (e.g. Empire, Liberty, C1 etc.) allowing design variations to be in close proximity. It has not been my intention to follow any chronological pattern with regard to construction dates. Brief tabular details are presented for selected ships of each type featured.

It was my late father, Chester Young, who passed the love of these ships to me, when I was just a lad. Len Sawyer (London) has been my closest friend, photographic partner and support for 30 years. He has allowed me to draw from his vast knowledge of these ships. My gratitude to him has no limit. All the photographs in this book are taken from original material, within the V. H. Young/L. A. Sawyer Photographic Collection.

I would also like to acknowledge the assistance I have received from Captain Walter Jaffee (U.S.A.), George Lamuth (U.S.A.), Mike McGarvey (U.S.A.), Warwick Foote (Australia), the late Fred Sankoff (Canada), Robert Head (New Zealand), all have helped in many ways. To my wife Niborom and our son Chester, go my love and heartfelt thanks for their years of support.

Victor Young, Wellington, New Zealand

June 1996

ANTIOPE 1941   **Anglo-Swiss Maritime Co. Ltd.**   *Panama*

One of seven Empire tramps built by Barclay, Curle & Co. Ltd., Glasgow, *Antiope* was completed in June 1941 as the *Empire Faith* and managed by Ellerman Lines. In 1946, renamed *Jessmore*, she came under the ownership of Johnson Warren Lines. The name *Antiope* was carried from 1958 until 1964 when Hong Kong owners, Wah Kwong, purchased and renamed her *Global Venture*. On 3 June 1971 she departed Hong Kong for her final voyage to shipbreakers at Kaohsiung.

This 1960 view shows her virtually unchanged from her wartime days, with perhaps, one significant difference. From mid-1940 the British war effort was turned towards winning the 'Battle of the Atlantic' as German bomber groups began operating from bases along, virtually, the whole coastline of western Europe. Their successful Kondor aircraft, searching for shipping targets, sank, in the six months to February 1941 alone, 85 Allied ships. It was obvious that effective protection of Allied

shipping could only be given by ship-borne fighter planes. But the Royal Navy's resources were already fully stretched and so Hawker Hurricane fighters were modified for rocket-propelled launching from catapults fitted atop merchant ships' bows. After some experiments 35 vessels, classified as CAM-ships (Catapult-Armed Merchantmen) were so fitted and put to sea. The *Empire Faith* was one. Twelve of the CAM-ships were lost. By June 1943 the remainder were redundant and phased out. Two sister ships were *Empire Highway* (Blue Star Line's *Ionic Star/Napier Star*) and *Empire Glade* (Ulster SS Co.'s *Inishowen Head*), although these were not CAM-ships.

Length	432' 00"	Gross tons	7,061
Beam	57' 05"	Engines	Oil 2SA 4cy
Draught	27' 06"		

SOUTHERN STAR 1947   **Bacong Shipping Co. S.A.**   *Panama*

The prototype for the ten Empire heavy lift ships was the 1926 built ***Belpareil*** of 7,203 gross tons. She was built for Christen Smith & Co., Oslo who were involved in the lifting of heavy cargoes via their company, Belships Co. Ltd. Vickers-Armstrongs Ltd., Barrow were given the task of taking the Norwegian design and adapting it for wartime construction. The first of the modified design, ***Empire Elaine***, was completed in 1942. The three large, unobstructed holds were each served by a 120 ton derrick. Well deck lengths were 78' 09" for'ard and 162' 02" aft. Vickers-Armstrongs Ltd. completed four ships at Barrow, with two more coming from their yard at Newcastle.

    Empire Canute was one of the four built by the Greenock Dockyard Co. Ltd. Launched on 24 December 1945, it was not until June 1947 that she was completed as ***Belocean*** for Belships Co. Ltd., registered in Oslo. In 1964 the flag of Norway was changed for that of Panama, to

go with the name ***Southern Star***. Bacong Shipping Co. S.A. was itself owned by Southern Industrial Projects Inc., Manila. It is interesting to note that this Philippine company, founded in 1962, also operated two other Empire heavy lift ships, ***Southern Comet*** ex ***Empire Byng*** and ***Southern Cross*** ex ***Empire Ethelbert***. From 1968 the ***Southern Star*** traded as the ***Marie Ann*** for Manila Interocean Lines Inc., Manila. 29 July 1976 saw her arrive at Gadani Beach, near Karachi, where shipbreakers ended her life of 30 years. She is shown here in Canadian waters in 1964.

Length	469' 10"	Gross tons	7,801
Beam	66' 10"	Engines	Steam turbine
Draught	26' 07"		connected to electric
			motor (original)
			Oil 2SA 8cy (1954)

GIANFRANCO 1944
Com. Italiana Transporti Maritimi
Italy

A 1961 photo showing **Gianfranco** under a heavy grey sky. One of the Empire "B" type, she was built by Short Brothers at Sunderland, which was also her port of registry. As **Empire Stuart**, she was managed by Strick Line. The wartime management of ships owned by The Ministry of War Transport was always a fickle affair. Management was often transferred from one shipping company to another, often on a voyage by voyage basis, depending on cargo and destination etc. **Empire Stuart**'s first post war owner was Ships Finance & Management Co., London. Renamed **Lord Lloyd George** she formed part of their fleet for nine years, 1947 to 1955, tramping worldwide.

A change of nationality came in 1955 when she became the **Atje-Ray-S**, owned by N. V. Rotterdamsche Kolen Centrale, Holland and registered at Rotterdam. From 1957 she took her final name **Gianfranco** and traded, as we see her here, until sold to Italian shipbreakers at Vado in late 1964. Many "B" type Empires served British owners post war; e.g. **Empire Southey** (**Hollybank**/Bank Line), **Empire Pickwick** (**Clan Mackendrick**/Clan Line) and **Empire Lady** (**Tweed**/Royal Mail Lines).

Length	446' 06"	Gross tons	6,971
Beam	56' 04"	Engines	T 3cy
Draught	26' 09"		

ALCYONIS 1944

Herculiania Maritime Co. Ltd.   *Greece*

Alcyonis was one of a large number of ships, of standard design, built during the war years on direct contract to an established shipowner. As a result, they were named in accordance with the owner's practice. Names prefixed **Empire** indicated Ministry of War Transport ownership, but with operational management put in the hands of established owners. *Alcyonis* was launched on 8 February 1944, at Sunderland, from the yard of William Doxford. She was completed in June 1944 as the **Trevethoe** for the well known tramp operator, Hain SS Co.

Two Hain sisters, **Trevose** and **Tresillian**, were also completed by Doxford in 1944. **Tresillian** spent the first few months of her life as Strick Line's **Registan** before being purchased by Hain SS Co. Other sisters included **Welsh Prince** (Prince Line), **Roybank** (Bank Line) and **Brockleymoor** (Runciman). Comparison of this 1963 photo with a wartime view reveals almost no change. Washports, ventilators, masting, flying bridge etc. are all as built. Interesting features are the small wheelhouse windows, standard on most warbuilt tonnage. These would have originally been fitted with shades or shutters. Wartime bridges were usually protected from air attack and splinters by the use of concrete reinforcing. As completed, four lifeboats were fitted instead of the two seen here. After ten years with her Greek owners, *Alcyonis* arrived at Kaohsiung, and the 'breakers yard, on 13 August 1969.

Length	444' 11"	Gross tons	7,365
Beam	56' 06"	Engines	Oil 3cy
Draught	27' 05"		

CAMPOS 1941

Cia. Nav. Campos

Panama

The **Empire Moon** was the fifth Empire tramp to come from J. L. Thompson's North Sands Shipyard at Sunderland. Launched on 15 December 1940, she was completed in May the following year. On 22 July 1943 while off Sicily, the **Empire Moon** was hit by a torpedo from **U-81**. Badly damaged, she was towed to Syracuse and beached. A report dated 9th June 1945 states that the **Empire Moon** had been refloated and would be discharged. On 13 June another report said that all compartments were dry, except for No.1, which was open to the sea. The **Empire Moon** left Syracuse in tow on 21 July 1945 and the following day arrived at Palermo, where permanent repairs were made. At the time of the 1943 attack she had been loaded with coal, destined for use as bunkers by the coal-burning ships taking part in "Operation Husky". Sold in 1949, she was renamed **Ionian Moon**, owned by Mediterranean SS Co. Ltd., London.

In 1953 ownership passed to Sterling Shipping Co. Ltd., Bahamas (A. Vergottis Ltd.), and she became the **Sterling Victory**. She was renamed **Alma** in 1957, under the Liberian flag, before finally becoming the **Campos** eleven years later. On 3 July 1969, a grey, overcast day, a group of ship photographers were on the New Waterway, Rotterdam. Suddenly an old ship was coming out of the greyness towards us. "It's an Empire", someone shouted. No time to check the camera. A few quick shots and she was passing . Grey sky, grey water, little noise, just the "Flop..Flop..Flop" of her prop as she "paddled" up to Rotterdam. We never saw the **Campos** again. She was scrapped at Shanghai in 1970.

Length	443' 08"	Gross tons	7,401
Beam	59' 11"	Engines	T 3cy
Draught	27' 00"		

LA BAHIA 1940   **Buries Markes Ltd**.   *London*

Photographed in 1961, almost at the end of five years with Buries Markes, *La Bahia* was launched on 26 February 1940 from William Doxford's Pallion yard at Sunderland. As the **Sutherland** she was completed in May 1940 for Newcastle owners, B. J. Sutherland. It was not until 13 January 1954 that she was sold to Chapman and Willan, becoming their third **Grainton**. She finally left the British register in 1961, when Buries Markes sold *La Bahia* to Valerosa Cia. Naviera S.A., Panama.

Renamed **San John**, she flew the Lebanese flag. Some 20 miles NW of Churchill, Hudson Bay, she ran aground on 4 October 1961 while on passage Tyne/Churchill. Refloated the next day, she was declared a constructive total loss. However, repairs were made, and **San John**

resumed tramping. *Ledra* was her name after sale to Atlas Shipping & Trading Co. Ltd., Cyprus, in 1965. This company was within the operation of London-based Greek owners, M. J. Lemos & Co. Ltd.

On a voyage from Madras to Poland with a cargo of iron ore she ran aground, 11 November 1967, on Alphee Shoal, Sri Lanka. Abandoned by the crew, who made the nearby shore without casualty, *Ledra* broke in two. Looted, and with the accommodation burnt out, the wreck was abandoned to the sea.

Length	442' 11"	Gross tons	5,172
Beam	56' 06"	Engines	Oil 2SA 3cy
Draught	25' 11"		

HORORATA 1942   **New Zealand Shipping Co. Ltd.**   *London*

Hororata was delivered to the New Zealand Shipping Co. by John Brown & Co. Ltd., Clydebank in April 1942. A simplified version of the Federal SN Co.'s **Essex** (1936), **Sussex** (1937) and **Suffolk** (1939), her hull measurements were almost identical to the earlier Federal ships. However, her superstructure was one deck lower and she was without a mainmast. *Hororata*'s eventful career started early. 13 December 1942 saw her homeward bound from Lyttelton for Liverpool, with a full cargo for war torn Britain. North of the Azores and in gale conditions, the *Hororata* was torpedoed by *U-103*. Because of her speed the ship was sailing without convoy or escort. The torpedo struck on the port side. Her Master and crew showed great seamanship in working the slowly sinking ship to an anchorage at Santa Cruz Bay, Flores Island. It was then decided to make for Horta, Fayal Island and the *Hororata* sailed after dark on 17 December, on the dangerous 150 mile passage. She arrived the following day.

Over the next three months an epic salvage operation was carried out in the harbour. Cargo was discharged, local timber felled for patches and 320 tons of concrete poured. On 17 March 1943 *Hororata* resumed her voyage to Liverpool, escorted by H.M.S. **Burwell**. She arrived on 23 March, with 10,000 tons of the original 11,300 ton cargo being delivered. Permanent repairs were carried out and in September 1943 she was ready for sea again. The **Hororata** is seen here at Wellington in June 1966. Sold in 1967, she was renamed **Nor** for a final voyage to the shipbreakers at Kaohsiung.

Length	551' 04"	Gross tons	12,090
Beam	70' 05"	Engines	6 x steam
Draught	32' 06"		turbine. twin
			screw

BENLARIG 1944

Ben Line Steamers Ltd.

Leith

Stumps fore and aft and a pole mast above the bridge. So often the trademark of warbuilt tonnage, these features are seen again in this view of **Benlarig** off Dock Head, Southampton on 27 August 1967. Built at Glasgow, by Blythswood Shipbuilding Co. Ltd., she was completed as **Javanese Prince** for Rio Cape Line, part of the Furness Withy group of companies. In 1954 ownership changed, within the group, to Prince Line. Later renamed **Benlarig**, she was part of the Ben Line fleet from 1961 until her arrival at Hong Kong, for scrapping, on 6 September 1969. Leung Yau Shipbreaking Co. were reported to have paid £48,000 for her. **Javanese Prince** came from a Silver Line (shipping company) design.

A sister ship, **Benvannoch**, was part of the Ben Line fleet until sold to Taiwanese shipbreakers in 1969. Built by J. L. Thompson & Sons Ltd., Sunderland in 1944 as the **Silveroak**, her sale to Ben Line in 1956

came after a 1955–56 charter to Port Line, with the name **Port Stephens**. Ben Line Steamers Ltd. was formed in 1919 by William Thomson & Co., Edinburgh, steamship operators since 1871. The United Kingdom to the Far East was their main trading route. By tradition, Hong Kong Chinese were employed as catering and engine room ratings. Appearance of the Ben Line ships always reflected the highest degree of maintenance. It was not uncommon to see the exterior steelwork on the superstructure hand painted to resemble a polished and panelled wood surface. One might assume that this was the artistry of the Chinese painter that many of the ships carried.

Length	482' 04"	Gross tons	8,879
Beam	62' 03"	Engines	Oil 2 6cy
Draught	29' 01"		

BENHIANT 1943

Ben Line Steamers Ltd.

Leith

Apart from armament and liferafts, most of the original features of the Empire "Standard Fast" type can be seen in this July 1969 view of the **Benhiant** ex **Empire Regent**, berthed in Liverpool. The ships were designed for speed and with an eye to post war trading. Accommodation was arranged in a high centre castle, leaving ample space for a deck cargo that might include locomotives, heavy military and industrial equipment. Cargo handling gear included 30, 50 and 80 ton derricks, served by electric winches. The traditional riveted lap plates can be clearly seen in this photo.

Fourteen ships of this type were completed by six shipyards between 1943 and 1946. Furness Shipbuilding Co. Ltd., Haverton Hill-on-Tees completed two, **Empire Chieftain** in October 1943 and **Empire Regent** the following month. An association with the waters "East of Suez" started early for the **Empire Regent**, when T. & J. Brocklebank became

her first wartime managers. In 1946 she was sold to Rio Cape Line (Furness Withy group), and renamed **Black Prince**. From 1949 until 1952 Shaw Savill took her on charter, using the name **Zealandic**. As the **Beaverlodge**, she was part of the fleet of Canadian Pacific Steamships Ltd., Liverpool, from 1952 until being sold to Ben Line in 1960. Cypriot operators Witty Compania Naviera S.A. took her away from the Red Ensign in 1970 and traded her for a year as the **Venus**. In this, her final year, she tramped worldwide, visiting Havana, Shimonoseki, Constantza and Lagos. Chuang Kuo Steel & Iron Works, Kaohsiung took delivery of her during July 1971 for scrapping.

Length	497' 07"	Gross tons	9,777
Beam	64' 05"	Engines	2 x steam
Draught	28' 02"		turbine

RUTHENIC 1944

Shaw Savill & Albion Ltd.

London

An unusual, heavy looking ship, **Ruthenic** was delivered from Harland & Wolff's Queen's Island yard, Belfast in December 1944, with the name **Durango**. A sister, **Drina**, was delivered from the same yard five months earlier. They were the second pair of four "D" class ships built during the war for Royal Mail Lines Ltd. The first pair, **Darro** and **Deseado**, differed in having a composite superstructure, No.3 hold being for'ard of the bridge. It could be said that the roots of their design came from the pre war "Highland" ships. Vertical bows, lack of sheer and squat funnel/s were features carried from the earlier Nelson/Royal Mail ships.

Durango spent most of her life in the frozen meat trade between U.K. and the River Plate. Vessels of this type were considered "heavy" ships by the deck crew, the large number of derricks, served by 19 winches, demanded a great deal of work. In 1966, on Shaw Savill charter, she made an eventful voyage to New Zealand. The **Durango** sailed from Wellington on Thursday, 3 February 1966 homeward bound to U.K. The following day, when 62 miles out of port, shots were fired in the crew quarters. **Durango** returned to Wellington and was boarded by police. A steward was rushed to hospital for surgery and another was charged with attempted murder. Later that year she was transferred to Shaw Savill and renamed, **Ruthenic**. Her short career with Shaw Savill ended after sale to Taiwanese 'breakers in 1967. She is shown here arriving at Wellington, 27 February 1967. War built ships of similar design were Houlder Line's **Rippingham Grange** and **Condesa**.

Length	468' 10"	Gross tons	9,801
Beam	65' 02"	Engines	Oil 2DA 6cy.
Draught	26' 10"		twin screw

WAIWERA 1944
Shaw Savill & Albion Ltd.
London

A strong northerly winds whips Wellington harbour on Saturday, 18 February 1967. The **Waiwera** sails for other New Zealand ports to complete discharge of her cargo from the United Kingdom. The stevedores and dock labour had finished working cargo in the late morning. The crew had then "turned to", stowing the derricks and cleaning down the weather decks. Next pre-sailing event was a large party for the deck, catering and engine room ratings and their shoreside lady friends. The pilot arrived at mid afternoon to a very festive scene. A makeshift bar, for crew and visitors, had been set up on the wharf. Empty food containers, bottles and toilet roll streamers added to the atmosphere of the summer party. In this case, if the view on this page was a picture of sound as well as vision, it could tell so much more!

This was almost at the end of **Waiwera**'s career. Later in 1967 she was sold to Greek owners, Embajada Cia. Nav. S.A. and renamed **Julia** for a one way voyage to Taiwanese shipbreakers. The vessel was reported to have arrived at Kaohsiung on 13 January 1968. Although a product of austere wartime conditions, **Waiwera** was of a design that had evolved from Shaw Savill's first motorships, **Coptic**, **Karamea**, **Zealandic** and **Taranaki**, built in 1928. The design was developed further in the mid 1930s with the completion by Harland and Wolff, Belfast of **Waiwera(II)**, **Waipawa**, **Wairangi**, **Waimarama** and **Waiotira**. When built, **Waiwera** had accommodation for 112 passengers. This was later removed.

Length	540' 00"	Gross tons	11,138
Beam	70' 06"	Engines	2 x Oil 6cy.
Draught	29' 07"		twin screw

RICHMOND CASTLE 1944   Union Castle Mail Steamship Co. Ltd.

Some 1960s colour film delivered a result other than expected. This 1968 view of the *Richmond Castle* in Rotterdam has the warmth of a desert sunset. The *Richmond Castle*, built under austere wartime conditions, continued the development of the Union Castle "R" class ships. The series had begun in 1935 with the delivery of two ships, *Roslin Castle*, of 443 feet, and the almost identical *Rothesay Castle*. The class was quickly developed and the slightly larger *Rochester, Roxburgh, Richmond* and *Rowallan Castle*'s were also in service by late 1939. Operating between U.K. and South Africa, the ships provided an express refrigerated service, without the timetable constraints that governed Union Castle passenger services. The *Rothesay Castle* was wrecked on the west coast of Scotland in January 1940 and by February 1943 the *Roxburgh, Richmond* and *Rowallan Castle*'s had been lost by enemy action. In August 1942 the *Rochester Castle* was part of "Operation Pedestal", the epic convoy to Malta.

Rowallan Castle (II), completed in 1943, was the first of the warbuilt ships, followed by *Richmond Castle (II)* and *Roxburgh Castle* in 1945. The series was completed the following year with the delivery of *Riebeeck* and *Rustenburg Castle*'s, slightly different ships, each having a composite superstructure with No.3 hold forward of the bridge. As built, the *Richmond Castle* was without topmasts but carried a signal mast above the bridge. The eleven ships were all built by Harland & Wolff at Belfast. The *Roslin Castle* was scrapped in 1967, *Rochester Castle* in 1970 and the warbuilt ships the following year. On 27 August 1971 the *Richmond Castle* arrived at Shanghai for delivery to Chinese shipbreakers.

Length	474' 02"	Gross tons	7,960
Beam	64' 04"	Engines	Oil 2DA 8cy
Draught	29' 03"		

ADEN 1946

P. & O. SN Co. Ltd.

London

Although not completed until September 1946 the *Aden*, originally named *Somerset*, was very much a product of austere wartime conditions. She had six sisters within the New Zealand Shipping Co./Federal SN fleets. All, including the *Somerset*, were built by Alexander Stephen & Sons Ltd., Linthouse, Glasgow. The *Gloucester* (see cover photo) and *Nottingham* (sunk by *U-74* on maiden voyage) were completed in 1941. *Papanui, Paparoa* and *Pipiriki* followed in 1943, then *Devon* and *Somerset* in 1946. The increasing use of welding in the shipbuilding industry resulted in the stern plating of both the *Devon* and *Somerset* differing from the earlier ships, their butt-welded plates resulting in a hard chine stern. The earlier ships were completed with a stern of conventional rolled plates.

In 1954 the *Somerset* was transferred to P.& O. SN Co. Ltd. and renamed *Aden*. On 8 October 1967 she arrived at Kaohsiung for breaking up. This 1964 view of the *Aden* clearly shows the butt-welded stern plates, so unusual for British war-designed ships of this size. Her signal mast also carries the MANZ Line flag. Montreal, Australia, New Zealand Line (MANZ) was set up by several British shipowners to operate joint services from Australasia to Canadian ports. The ships were usually chartered from the fleets of the parent companies, e.g. Port Line, Blue Star, New Zealand Shipping Co.

Length	495' 04"	Gross tons	9,943
Beam	64' 10"	Engines	3 x steam
Draught	27' 04"		turbine

BRENT 1945

R. & J. Hall

Maldon, Essex

The story of the TID (Tug Inshore Dock) tugs is, in many ways, the saga of World War II shipbuilding in capsular form. A drastic wartime shortage of small harbour tugs demanded an equally drastic and innovative building programme. To produce suitable vessels, in large numbers, plans were prepared for a prefabricated tug, suitable for mass production. All frame work would be built on the square and there would be a minimum of rolled steel plate. The 74ft hull was divided into eight sections, designed as independent units, to be constructed by subcontractors, who needed to be neither shipbuilders nor local to the assembly site. The subcontractors were to deliver sections with most hull and deck fittings in place. One hull was to be produced every five days. Richard Dunston Ltd. assembled the completed units in their shipyards at Thorne and Hessle in Yorkshire. Later in the programme Wm. Pickersgill & Sons Ltd., Sunderland also assembled vessels.

TID 1 was launched on 26 February 1943. Completed the following month, she was the first of an order for 182 vessels. Some of the construction methods were as radical as the design itself. Sections were delivered with unwelded seams at either end. This allowed for adjustment to units that were not exactly to plan length. The engine and tailshaft were aligned after launching, the engine bedplate being adjusted to suit variations in each hull. *TID 159* was completed by Wm. Pickersgill & Sons Ltd. Purchased by the Port of London Authority in 1947, she was renamed *Brent* in 1948. Sold for scrap in 1969, she was then reprieved in 1971, when resold to R. & J. Hall. The vessel is now in private use.

Length	73' 10"	Gross tons	54
Beam	17' 00"	Engine	Compound 2cy
Draught	8' 00"	Bollard pull	2 tons

NAPIA 1943

Ship Towage Ltd.

London

Napia was typical of the Empire tugs built in the U.K. during World War II. The output was divided into several classes. *Napia* was constructed by Goole Shipbuilding & Repair Co. Ltd., as **Empire Jester**. As the course of the war moved towards the Mediterranean, the demand for towage services increased. Salvage operations and general shiphandling in liberated ports required tugs of suitable range and size. Problems of supply ruled out the use of coal as fuel. Converting existing tugs to burn oil was undesirable and would have affected their stability.

The tug **Roach**, built in 1935, was used as a prototype for the new oilfired vessels. Developed from the earlier coal burning "Warrior" type, came 21 tugs of the "Modified-Warrior" design. *Napia* was one of them. The vessel was managed by United Towing Co. Ltd. of Hull until 1946, when purchased by William Watkins Ltd. of London and renamed **Napia**. She served on the Thames until 1971. During these

years there were changes of owner due to amalgamation within the towage industry. Greek owner John G. Efthinou operated her from 1971 until 1973, and then she passed to another Greek, Loucas G. Matsas. Her career ended on 19 February 1986 when demolition commenced at Perama. The name **Tolmiros** was carried for all of her fifteen years under the Greek flag. This 1969 view shows **Napia** outside the Royal Docks on the London River. The 'Royals' were a favourite area for ship photographers. Without realisation, we were photographing at the end of an era. The ships and the seafaring ways of our youth were soon to be replaced by the containers and container ships of today.

Length	114' 00"	Gross tons	261
Beam	30' 01"	Engines	T 3cy
Draught	12' 05"		

BAGAS 1946   **Bahari Bahtera P.T. Perusahan Pelayaran Nusantara**   *Indonesia*

Singapore, 24 February 1975. Almost unaltered after 29 years' service, the **Bagas** rides at anchor awaiting a discharge berth. It was a time when anchorages all over South East Asia were full of ships built or designed during, or before, the years of World War II.

    Bagas was delivered by the Goole Shipbuilding & Repair Co. Ltd. to the Bristol SN Co. Ltd. in April 1946. As the **Ino**, she served her original owners in the U.K. coastal trade for seven years. The Adelaide SS Co. Ltd. of Australia purchased her in December 1953. Renamed **Maltara** (after a type of Australian eucalyptus tree), cargoes of limestone, for the production of cement, provided regular employment. In 1967 she left the Australian coast, and renamed **Sandy**, traded for Asia-Africa Shipping Co., Hong Kong. Her move to South East Asia came in 1973. Still named **Sandy**, she operated for Unique Shipping & Trading Co. of Singapore, at

a time when the war in Vietnam was heading for its painful conclusion. Freight rates were high and many local owners were making good profits running small ships to high-risk ports such as Phnom Penh, Cambodia and Saigon, Vietnam. It was common to see these ships off Singapore, with sandbags and screens set up around the bridge, giving meagre protection from incoming rockets and mortar shells from both sides of the war zone rivers! Perhaps **Sandy** was involved in this trade. The ship was renamed **Bagas** in 1974. Further changes of ownership, within Indonesia, took place in 1976, and again in 1979. The vessel was reported scrapped in 1991.

Length	209' 04"	Gross tons	959
Beam	31' 05"	Engine	Oil 2SA 7cy
Draught	13' 07"		

Above The very last of the evening sun washes over the **Caledonia Star** as she pulls away from Aotea Quay, Wellington, on 9 February 1971. Ten months later she was delivered to shipbreakers at Kaohsiung. From this view it can be seen just how little she had changed. Although the wartime "woodbine" funnel was replaced she still looks every bit an Empire. Jumbo derrick over No.2 hold, wartime wheelhouse windows, signal mast, galley stovepipe, and wooden clinker lifeboats on original davits, all features direct from 1942.

CALEDONIA STAR A Photo Essay

A wartime development of a Clan Line design that started with the **Clan Cameron** in 1937. As **Empire Wisdom**, the **Caledonia Star** was completed by the Greenock Dockyard Co. Ltd. in November 1942, along with sister ship **Empire Might**. Management was transferred from Clan to Blue Star Line in 1944. As the **Royal Star** she became part of the Blue Star fleet in 1946.

Length	487' 07"	Gross tons	9,141	
Beam	63' 00"	Engines	T 6cy. twin screw	
Draught	29' 10"		Oil 2 x 5cyl (after 1961)	

Above   This view of the coal-fired galley comes complete with the roast meat for midday lunch sitting in the baking dish. An interesting feature is the riveted construction of bulkhead frames and deckhead. The galley was on the main deck just aft of No.3 hold.

Right   The old and the new. The horn of the electric whistle contrasts with the beautiful brass of, perhaps what could be, the original steam whistle. Lanyards for both have been laid slack to allow for the working of cargo at No.3.

MERCURY 1945   **Naviera Voluntad Soc. de R. L.**   *Honduras*

Mercury is an interesting example of British wartime prefabricated construction. There is an absence of sheer and rolled plating. The entry to the water of the bow section is formed with butt-welded, flat plate. One of the 'Shelt' type coasters, built for Far East service, she came from the yard of Henry Scarr Ltd., Hessle in June 1945 as **Empire Seabreeze**. The design was very similar to the "Chant" tankers and "Empire-F" type coasters, although the "Shelt" type were fitted with shelter decks and side doors.

    Eleven of the type were completed by Henry Scarr. Ten of these, including **Empire Seabreeze**, were purchased post war by Straits SS Co., who renamed her **Senai**. Straits SS Co. was a household name in South East Asia, with extensive local cargo and passenger services.

She served the company until becoming the **Changi** in 1962, with owners based in Hong Kong. Later in the same year there was another name change. Cosmos Shipping Co. S.A. of Panama renamed her **Mene**. It is almost certain that, throughout these changes of name and ownership, she continued to trade out of Singapore. The final name, **Mercury**, and the flag of Honduras, came in 1983. **Mercury** floundered off Tumpat, Malaysia, 23 December 1984. Reports state that this was caused by taking water in the engine room. She is seen here anchored off Singapore on 1 March 1983.

Length	148' 02"	Gross tons	522
Beam	27' 01"	Engines	Oil 2SA 4cy
Draught	10' 00"		

NUNEZ DE BALBOA 1942   Ramirez Escudero, Adolfo   *Bilbao, Spain*

In this 1961 photo the **Nunez De Balboa** carries the flag of Panama, a 'flag of convenience'. Her Spanish name is the only clue to the nationality of her owner. The vessel was registered under the ownership of Cia. Auxiliar Maritima Ltda, Port Limon, Costa Rica, a company formed in 1955, by her 'real' owner in Bilbao, Spain.

J. L. Thompson & Sons Ltd., North Sands Shipyard, Sunderland completed the **Thistlemuir** in 1942 for Allan, Black & Co. Ltd. Service under the Red Ensign ended in 1961, on becoming the **Nunez De Balboa**. She was sold to Japanese shipbreakers in 1968.

J. L. Thompson & Sons Ltd., and their shipyard at North Sands, could well be considered the parents and the birthplace of the whole World War II Allied merchant shipbuilding programme. During 1940, raiders and U-Boats were sinking merchant ships faster than British yards could replace them. In September of that year the British

Shipbuilding Mission, led by Mr Robert Cyril Thompson (a director of the Sunderland company), was sent to the U.S.A. to arrange the building of ships for British account. The plans taken were simplified drawings of the **Dorington Court**, a tramp built by the firm in 1938. The success of this mission resulted in the building of the 60 ships of the "Ocean" type. The same British plans were then developed into the American built Liberty Ship. The table below compares the U.S. built "Ocean" type (in brackets) with the Empire ship, **Nunez De Balboa**, and indicates the passage of design, from England to U.S.A. Both were children of Sunderland.

Length	441' 05"	(441' 06")	Gross tons	7,076	(7,174)
Beam	57' 02"	(57' 00")	Engines	T 3cy	
Draught	26' 11"	(26' 10")			

VIC 56   1945

J. H. Cleary

London

The VIC (Victualling Inshore Craft) lighter was the smallest of the coastal types adapted for a wartime mass building programme. From the outbreak of war the greatly increased activity at all Royal Navy facilities created the demand for a fleet of small coaster/lighter type vessels to service naval requirements. The ideal prototype was the Clyde "Puffer". The unusual nickname was derived from the unique engine noise that resulted from the direct exhaust of the simple steam engine, without a condenser. These small, flat bottomed vessels had long been used with great success on Scottish waterways and coastal services. Their dimensions were restricted by the size of the locks on the Forth and Clyde Canal. The Admiralty Merchant Shipping Department produced the plans for the VIC lighters, the wartime Clyde "Puffers".

VIC 1 was completed in November 1941 by Richard Dunston Ltd., Thorne, the first of an initial order for 64 vessels. The plans were developed

further and approximately 40 "Improved VIC Lighters" were built. These were larger vessels (original VIC length 66' 08"), with the funnel placed aft of the wheelhouse. *VIC 56*, one of the "Improved" type, was launched by J. Pollock & Sons Ltd., Faversham on 22 November 1945 and completed the following month. In 1947 her ownership passed from the Ministry of War Transport to the Admiralty and she was based at Rosyth. After being laid up for four years the ship was sold to M. Cleary of Wealdstone, Middlesex, and is now in private use in the London area. *VIC 32* (built 1943) is preserved at Ardrishaig, Scotland and used for steamboat cruising holidays, carrying twelve passengers. *VIC 96* (built 1945) is a museum ship at Maryport. *VIC 56* is seen here at Rochester, Kent on 1 July 1984.

Length	85' 00"	Gross tons	147
Beam	20' 00"	Engine	steam
Draught	8' 06"		compound

WAIHEMO 1944   **Union SS Co. of New Zealand Ltd.**   *Wellington, New Zealand*

West Coast S. B. Ltd., Vancouver launched the **Fort Mackinac (II)** in 1944, completing her in August of the same year, as the **Dominion Park**. At war's end she was operated by Canadian Australasian Line. This was a joint venture between the Union SS Co. of New Zealand Ltd. and Canadian Pacific. Along with four other Parks (**Waikawa/ Wairuna/Waitomo** and **Waitemata**) a cargo service was maintained from west coast Canadian and U.S. ports to New Zealand, via Pacific islands. A small number of passengers were also carried. Madrigal Shipping Co. Inc. of Manila purchased **Waihemo** in 1967, renaming her **Maria Susana**. The registered owner was Pac-Trade Nav. Co.,

Monrovia. Apart from briefly running aground in 1971, the next five years were spent tramping, uneventfully, in Asian and Australian waters. **Maria Susana** arrived at Kaohsiung for scrapping, 27 May 1972.

Here we see the **Waihemo** in the Floating Dock, Wellington, New Zealand, in August 1964. The dock itself was towed from England in 1931. Sold to Thai interests in 1988, it broke up and sank in the Tasman Sea on its delivery voyage to Bangkok, under tow.

Length	439' 04"	Gross tons	7,206
Beam	57' 02"	Engines	T 3cy
Draught	26' 11"		

OAK HILL 1943

Counties Ship Management Co. Ltd.

London

Counties Ship Management, the Red Ensign and the Canadian built Fort and Park types. The three would be synonymous in the minds of many who were involved in the shipping industry of the 1950–60s. The same could be said about the names Kulukundis, London, Overseas Freighters Ltd. and Mavroleon. This group of London based Greek owners operated a large fleet of World War II standards. Twenty-nine Fort/Park ships passed through their fleets, many named after London suburbs with the suffix *Hill*. In the 1960s, age and prohibitive insurance rates forced warbuilt tonnage out of commercial operation. This same group was responsible for the initial development of the SD14, a standard design tramp that became known, in the 1970s, as the "Liberty Replacement".

Oak Hill was completed in 1943 as the *Fort Michipicoten*, by Marine Industries Ltd., Sorel, Quebec. Chartered to the British Government, her managers included Maclay & Macintyre Ltd. and A.Crawford & Co.Ltd. She became the *Oak Hill* in 1950. Aegis Shipping Co. Ltd. of Greece purchased and renamed her *Agenor* in 1964. Her final commercial voyage was from Nakhodka to Colombo, arriving there on 11 September 1968. Sold to Chinese breakers, she departed for Whampoa. The vessel developed a serious leak in the engine room and was towed into Singapore on 6 November 1968. Unconfirmed reports indicate that demolition took place there. This September 1961 photo of *Oak Hill* shows a standard of upkeep to rival many liner companies.

Length	441' 07"	Gross tons	7,139
Beam	57' 02"	Engines	T 3cy
Draught	26' 10"		

ZINNIA 1945

Stag Line Ltd.

North Shields

The Battle of the Atlantic had passed its darkest months, the tide had turned. Merchant shipbuilding programmes were in place and well established in Britain, the U.S.A. and Canada. It was 1945, resources were being channelled to the Pacific war zone. There was a need for maintenance and repair ships to support the Allied fleet, island hopping towards Japan. Twenty-one Maintenance and Repair ships were ordered, within the Canadian Fort/Park building programme. *Zinnia* was built by the Burrard DD Co. Ltd., Vancouver as the armament maintenance ship H.M.S. *Portland Bill*, although not completed until December 1945. After purchase by Stag Line in 1951, and conversion in the UK, *Zinnia* traded for the company for the next thirteen years.

This 1962 photo shows that the post war rebuilding retained all the features of the basic Fort/Park ships, the only difference being that No.3 hold has been trunked through extended main deck accommodation. Astrosuerte Cia. Nav. S.A., Liberia renamed her *Chrysopolis* in 1965. On 18 May 1965 she arrived at Kaohsiung for scrapping. Examples of similar conversions were *Waitemata* (Union SS Co. Ltd., New Zealand), *Dongola* (P. & O. SN Co. Ltd.) and *Lakemba* (Pacific Shipowners, Fiji).

Length	441' 06"	Gross tons	7,292
Beam	57' 02"	Engines	T 3cy
Draught	27' 09"		

Above A moment of triumph. After 33 years laid up, ***Jeremiah O'Brien*** steams out of Suisun Bay.

JEREMIAH O'BRIEN A Photo Essay

The Liberty Ship. Perhaps more than any other type, the Liberty epitomises every aspect of merchant shipbuilding in World War II. The vision and genius of British design. The enormity and unmatched ability of American industry. These factors together created the greatest shipbuilding programme the world has ever seen, the Liberty Fleet. ***Jeremiah O'Brien*** is one of that fleet . One of the 2,710 Liberty ships built during World War II.

New England Shipbuilding Corp. built the ***Jeremiah O'Brien*** at their West Yard in South Portland, Maine. She was delivered to Grace Line Inc., her managers, on 30 June 1943. Seven wartime voyages took her from the North Atlantic and the Normandy landings, to the Philippines, Shanghai and Calcutta. Early in 1946 she entered the U.S. Reserve Fleet at Suisun Bay, California. In the years that followed her commercial sisters traded worldwide. Liberty ships

also became fish factories in Alaska, Radar Pickets for the U.S. Navy, test ships for gas turbine propulsion, even a floating nuclear power plant. By the mid 1960s, however, it was clear that their commercial and strategic value was almost gone. Liberties were stripped from the U.S. reserve fleets. Some were sunk as environmental fish reefs, others, loaded with obsolete ammunition and chemicals, were treated the same way. Most were scrapped.

Jeremiah O'Brien, still in her original condition, remained. There were those within the U.S. Maritime Administration who realised her value: her potential to be preserved as a working memorial to the standard merchant ships of World War II. In 1978, the National Liberty Ship Memorial, Inc., a California based, non-profit corporation was formed. That same year, ***Jeremiah O'Brien*** was declared a U.S. National Monument and thus registered as an "historic place".

At her lay-up location, a group of volunteers worked under the most adverse conditions to bring the ship to life again. On 6 October 1979, after more than 33 years laid up, the ***Jeremiah O'Brien*** steamed out of Suisun Bay under her own power. The Bethlehem Steel Shipyard in San Francisco assisted the volunteers in a major programme of restoration and activation. The first Annual Seaman's Memorial Cruise, in San Francisco Bay, took place 21 May 1980. Since that time the ship has maintained a regular cruise calendar as well as weekend open days. She is a tribute to her design, builder and those who fought so hard to preserve her.

Another Liberty, the ***John W. Brown***, has now been preserved at Baltimore on the U.S. east coast. Her restoration and operation is in the hands of "Project Liberty Ship", also a volunteer group. She served as a maritime school ship at New York between 1945 and 1982. After a short period in the James River Reserve Fleet, a programme to preserve her began in 1983. Several memorial cruises have been completed and public open days are held regularly. A well-produced newsletter, *The Ugly Duckling* is published for crew, friends and supporters around the world.

Above Decked in flags, bathed in sunlight, the ***O'Brien*** cruises San Francisco Bay, 17 May 1987.

S.S. JEREMIAH O'BRIEN
BUILT FOR
U.S. MARITIME COMMISSION
HULL NO. 230
BY
NEW ENGLAND SHIPBUILDING CO.
SOUTH PORTLAND, MAINE
JUNE 1943

Above The **Jeremiah O'Brien** provides a backdrop for a brass and drum band during "D-Day" commemoration events in the Southampton Docks, Saturday, 4 June 1994.

In 1994 the **Jeremiah O'Brien** completed a voyage that many thought could not be done. It was said that she had an "Appointment in Normandy". Departing San Francisco on 18 April 1994, an epic five-and-a-half-month voyage began. Through the Panama Canal and across the Atlantic to the "D-Day" beaches of France. Captain George Jahn was Master, with Captain Walter W. Jaffee, his Chief Mate. Landfall at the Lizard (the south west tip of England) was made on 21 May. President Clinton, in Europe for the "D-Day" commemorations, visited the ship when she was at anchor in the Solent. Addressing the crew, the President said "This is a great day for the Merchant Marine. I'm proud to be

on board. Thank you for what you have done." A call at Southampton preceded the **Jeremiah O'Brien**'s return to France on 6 June 1994. Chatham, London, Cherbourg, Rouen and Le Havre were visited before recrossing the Atlantic to her birthplace at Portland, Maine. Calls at Baltimore, Jacksonville and another Panama Canal transit completed the round voyage at San Francisco, on 23 September 1994. Two Atlantic crossings, 18,000 miles, a crew with an average age of 70 and a 50 year old ship in ballast trim. The spirit that built the Liberty fleet lives on. It is certain that Robert Cyril Thompson and Henry J. Kaiser would have smiled and said "WELL DONE!"

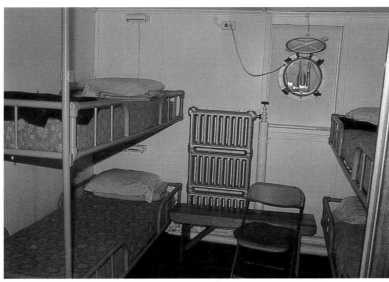

Top   Visitors board the ship in Chatham Dockyard, 12 June 1994.
Above   Located aft, accommodation for the gun crew.

Right   The foremast.

O. B. MARTIN 1944   **U.S. Department of Commerce**   *U.S.A.*

This bow view illustrates the appearance of a Liberty after many years in the reserve fleet. *O. B. Martin* is a time capsule going back to May 1944 and her completion by Todd Houston Shipbuilding Corp., Houston, Texas. Apart from the removal of armament, she is exactly as built. The wartime concrete splinter shield around the bridge and wheelhouse can be clearly seen. Although faded, the commercial funnel marking would indicate that, just after the war, she was operated by Luckenbach Steamship Co. Inc. In distress, she put into Port Elizabeth on 26 December 1944. Her cargo of coal had shifted. Apart from that minor incident, *O. B. Martin* is a ship that has left little behind to mark her existence.

In this March 1973 photo she waits at Pier 36, San Francisco for the arrival of the tug which was to tow her to Taiwan for scrapping. The white "V" painted on the stem could be considered a trademark of reserve fleet ships. Should the "V" submerge, tank soundings would be taken to locate a leak or the cause of increased draught. Checks such as this were part of the daily duties of the reserve fleet service crews. It was common for a reserve fleet to have a comprehensive support facility on site, including workshops, storage, administration offices, pontoons and tugs. On many ships the accommodation was sealed. Shoreside power, by way of cable, was used to run humidity control units placed on board each ship, with the indicators mounted on the inside of selected portholes. These would be monitored by service teams making regular visits. Ships of the U.S. reserve fleet were maintained in a state that would allow for quick reactivation.

Standard Liberty ship data is:

Length	441' 06"	Gross tons	7,176
Beam	57' 00"	Engines	T 3cy
Draught	27' 09"		

HELLENIC WAVE 1943   P. G. Callimanopulos   *Piraeus, Greece*

This 1964 photograph of the **Hellenic Wave** certainly reflects the very high standard of maintenance that was common to all units of the Callimanopulos fleet. The company was formed in 1920 and later established offices in New York. Hellenic Lines, operators of the **Hellenic Wave**, was one of several managing companies within the group. Other World War II standard types were also operated. **John Ross** was completed by the Permanente Metals Corporation, Yard No.2, Richmond, California, July 1943. Sold by the War Shipping Administration in 1947, the purchaser was Callimanopulos. As **Hellenic Wave**, she remained with the company for the next 22 years.

In 1970, after sale to Canopus Shipping of Greece, she was registered at Famagusta, Cyprus, managed by Pollux Shipping Co.Ltd. and renamed **Aghios Ermolaos**. Her final commercial voyage came in mid 1973. This was from Samsun, on the Black Sea, to Rosario, Argentina,

returning to Venice. The next voyage, under tow, was to Spanish shipbreakers at Castellon in August 1973.

The Liberty Ship was given the U.S. Maritime Commission code EC2-S-C1. EC stood for Emergency Cargo, 2 indicated the size of the vessel in relation to USMC coding, S referred to steam propulsion and C1 gave the design, in relation to the other indicators.

The first Liberty ship built was the **Patrick Henry**. Delivered from the Bethlehem Fairfield Shipyard, Baltimore on 30 December 1941, she survived the war and was scrapped in 1958. The record for the fastest building time goes to the Permanente Metals Corporation, Yard No.2, Richmond, California. In November 1942 they sent the **Robert E. Peary** on sea trials, less than eight days after the laying of her keel. She was scrapped in 1963.

For standard Liberty ship data, see page 32.

VALLSUN 1943

Intrafina Ltd.

London

For the Allies, 1942 was the worst year in the Battle of the Atlantic. The German command had developed the U-Boat Wolf Pack operation almost to an art form. Merchant ship losses were at their highest and the full benefits of wartime shipbuilding programmes had yet to be seen. Urgent action was needed. An emergency tanker was designed, by Delta Shipbuilding Co., New Orleans, using the Liberty hull. A total of 62 were built. The dry cargo spaces and bulkheads were redesigned for bulk petroleum products. The Liberty tankers, in outward appearance, were very similar to the dry cargo ships. Dummy cargo gear, concealed deck piping and oil hatches were fitted. The oil tanks were vented through the masts. It was a clever deception, giving the tankers anonymity within the convoy system.

Vallsun was built as the Liberty tanker ***Andrew Marschalk*** in 1943 by Delta Shipbuilding Co. Sold to U.S. operators in 1948, her first name change came in 1950 when Orion Shipping & Trading Co. Inc., New York renamed her ***Seaglorious***. Conversion to dry cargo took place in 1955. The following year she was converted to an ore carrier, lengthened and renamed ***Andros Glider***. Ownership was still within the Orion Shipping & Trading group of companies when she became the ***Evrotas*** in 1960. The names ***Kini***, ***Three Sisters*** and ***Kriti*** followed until becoming the ***Vallsun*** in 1973. The following year she was sold to Taiwanese shipbreakers.

Length	511' 06"	Gross tons	8,433
Beam	57' 00"	Engines	T 3cy
Draught	26' 03"		

CAPTAIN LEMOS 1943   **Lemos G. Brothers Co. Ltd.**   *London*

Well down to her marks with a grain cargo, the *Captain Lemos* prepares to leave Canadian waters in this 1965 view. Twenty-two years before, in August 1943, she had been completed as the *Arthur P. Davis*, by California Shipbuilding Corp., Terminal Island, Los Angeles. Known as 'Calship', the Corporation delivered 306 Liberty ships, 30 Liberty tankers and then constructed Victory ships. Managed by American West African Line Inc., New York, she retained her original name until her sale in 1947. Renamed **North Valley**, she was operated by Norton Lilley Management Corp., New York until being sold again in 1950. A third owner, Orion Shipping & Trading Co. Inc., New York, renamed her **Andre**. The Stars and Stripes were replaced by the flag of Panama. Ten years later she became the *Captain Lemos*. Her last "finished with engines" was rung down on delivery to Shanghai shipbreakers, on 12 February 1968.

An interesting feature in this photo is the crack arrestor plate. Riveted to the hull, outboard at main deck level, it extends from No.3 hold through to the aft end of No.4. These plates were also fitted on the main deck, especially in the area adjacent to the aft end of No.3 hatch. There were examples of Liberty ships breaking in two with claims of poor design, poor materials and substandard welding. Most of the reported failures involved ships that were operating in Arctic-like conditions. Investigations were made and changes carried out, including the addition of the crack arrestor plates. The molecular structure of the steel, used for new ships, was also altered to allow for low temperature operation. Wartime emergency demanded the speed of welded construction. The building of the Liberty fleet taught lessons that have contributed to today's universal acceptance of welding in the shipbuilding industry.

For standard Liberty ship data, see page 32.

AFRICAN NIGHT 1944   **Salvatores & C.S.R.L.**   *Genoa, Italy*

U.S. flag Liberty ships were named after deceased, notable Americans. This was a very broad policy. In general they were named for those who had made a substantial contribution to American sport, culture, art or history. Liberty ships were included in wartime Lend/Lease agreements between the U.S.A. and Great Britain. In this way, around 200 Liberty ships were transferred to British operators. Those completed for Britain received names prefixed **Sam**. This was a reflection of the British Ministry of War Transport's description of the Liberties as being ships with Superstructure Aft of Midships (SAM). In many cases these ships were first launched with American names. For generations of British seamen they were known as "The SAM Boats". **African Night** was a "Sam Boat".

Samtana, completed June 1944 by the Bethlehem Fairfield Shipyard at Baltimore, went directly to the management of Lyle Shipping Co. Ltd., Glasgow. As was often the case, management later became ownership. **Samtana** was purchased by Lyle Shipping Co. Ltd. and renamed **Cape Verde** in 1947. Ten years later she became the **African Night**. This view of her dates from 1961. It would appear that the funnel has been rebuilt, taller than the original and without the cowl top. She was sold to Taiwanese 'breakers and arrived at Kaohsiung on 26 June 1967.

For standard Liberty ship data, see page 32.

VOLGOGRAD 1944   **U.S.S.R. Merchant Marine**   Moscow

Liberty ships, sailing under the Soviet flag, were at sea until the mid 1970s. These were vessels that had been passed to Russia during the war under the terms of Lend/Lease. However, they were never returned nor paid for. This, despite requests from the U.S.A. for the matter to be addressed. This situation involved at least 38 ships. Over the years, most had a degree of rebuilding carried out to the bridge and wheelhouse. The original monkey island was plated in to create a new wheelhouse, thus creating a superstructure one deck higher than the original. This feature can be clearly seen in this photograph of the **Volgograd**, off Pulau Bukom, Singapore on 17 March 1974. A substantial pole mast has also been fitted above the bridge. The Permanente Metals Corporation (Yard No.2) launched the **Thomas M.**

Flaherty, completing her in April 1944 as the **Stalingrad**. It was not until 1962 that she was renamed **Volgograd**.

Into the1970s, as reports of Russian Liberty ship movements and sightings dwindled, their names were removed from Lloyd's Register. Some were converted for "non-transportation use", whilst others involved Liberty hulls being used as barges and floating accommodation units etc, in the Soviet Union. Mystery does not surround the fate of all, however. **Pskov** went to U.K. shipbreakers at Faslane in September 1970. **Sergei Kirov** and **Sukhona** were scrapped in Spain the following year. **Sovetskaya Gavan** was sold to Indian shipbreakers at Bombay in 1990. **Vitebsk** arrived at Kaohsiung for scrapping in July 1972.

For standard Liberty ship data, see page 32.

SANTA ELISABETTA 1943   Soc. Officiene G. Malvicini Vapori   *Genoa, Italy*

The New England Shipbuilding Corporation, South Portland, Maine built 244 Liberties. These included the **William Pitt Preble**, completed in November 1943 as the **Samrich**. The British Ministry of War Transport (M.O.W.T.) passed her management to Shaw Savill Line, London. Her first voyages were in the Mediterranean. She was part of the Allied supply train moving stores and equipment in support of the Italian landings. At Lourenco Marques, on 25 February 1944 survey work was carried out after the failure of a non-return valve resulted in some leaking in No.5 hold. Her next casualty required far greater repairs. On 12 April 1945 **Samrich** was anchored in Sea Reach, River Thames. At 1730 the Canadian built **Fort Caribou**, while swinging to come to anchor, collided with the **Samrich**. There was considerable damage to both ships. Bow damage to the **Samrich** involved frames and strakes, torn welding and a buckled collision bulkhead. **Fort Caribou** suffered

damage between hatches 4 and 5. Raft skids were fractured, starboard lifeboat was squeezed and the main deck was set up.

Shaw Savill Line purchased two Liberties in 1947. **Samrich** became the **Cufic**. **Samsylvan**, which the company had also managed for the M.O.W.T., was renamed **Tropic**. **Cufic** went to Italian buyers and was renamed **Santa Elisabetta** in 1953. This photo from 1965 shows her looking exactly as she did during her years with Shaw Savill. The extensive rebuilding of the monkey island and the taller than original funnel were early post war, Shaw Savill, modifications. In 1967, the final year of her life, she was renamed **Star**, under the flag of Panama, owned by Bluestar Enterprises Inc. This was a company set up by La Navale S.N.C., Genoa, Italy. **Star** sailed from Moji, Japan on 15 March 1968, on a final voyage to the scrapyard at Kaohsiung.

For standard Liberty ship data, see page 32.

THOMAS T. TUCKER 1942   **War Shipping Administration**   *U.S.A*

Dense fog and compass error combined to cause the grounding of the *Thomas T. Tucker*, near Cape Point, 54 miles from Cape Town, South Africa. This was during the early hours of 28 November 1942. Todd Houston Shipbuilding Corporation, Houston, Texas had delivered the *Thomas T. Tucker* only a month before. This maiden voyage was to have been from New Orleans to Suez, via Cape Town. Most of the cargo comprised heavy military equipment. The vessel struck a ledge of rock in way of No.3 hold. The hold and engine room quickly flooded. This, combined with the heavy cargo, made salvage prospects bleak from the outset. Tugs were sent from Cape Town. Over more than eight hours, repeated attempts to free her failed. The large swells of the exposed location caused her to pound, sealing her fate. Lighters were placed alongside in an effort to salvage some of the cargo. The 1942 built tug *Empire Goblin* was used by the South African Railways and Harbours Authority to tow the loaded lighters to Cape Town. The operation continued for two or three weeks until the ship, broken in three, was abandoned. Throughout there were no casualties.

On 26 August 1972, friends and I visited the wreck site. Bow and stern still carried the lines of a Liberty Ship. The midship section was a rusted mass of steel, without recognisable form. We collected small pieces of steel plate, enduring reminders of our visit. After almost 30 years of pounding, the sea had not altogether claimed the *Thomas T. Tucker*. Indeed a tribute to the Liberty ship, its strength and design.

For standard Liberty ship data, see page 32.

SAINT VALERY EN CAUX 1943   **French Government**   *Paris*

Soft evening light imparts a feeling of tranquillity to this 1962 view. *Saint Valery En Caux* was in the final months of her fourteen years under the French flag.

As the *George W. Campbell*, she was completed by the Oregon Shipbuilding Corp., Portland, Oregon in January 1943. Allied victory in North Africa resulted in large numbers of prisoners of war being transported to the U.S.A. *George W. Campbell* was one of the 157 Liberty ships converted to Limited Capacity troopships. She had accommodation for up to 504 prisoners in "5-high" berths. On return voyages she accommodated up to 350 U.S. troops, but in "3-high" berths. During a visit to New York in April 1944 she collided with the U.S. tug *Admiral Dewey*. The *George W. Campbell* was in the news again the following year. On 8 May 1945 she collided with the U.S.

flag Liberty, **Leonardo L. Romero**, off Portland, England. Plating on the port bow was torn for 20 feet, some below the waterline. On 10 May the *George W. Campbell* arrived at Southampton, sailing the next day for repairs at a Bristol Channel port. Purchased by the French Government in 1946, she was renamed *Saint Valery En Caux*. From 1949 the name was shortened to *St. Valery* by her managers at the time, Messageries Maritimes, Paris. The full name was restored in 1956. Six years later, Naviera y Financiera Ltda. of Lebanon renamed her **Henriette**. Sold to Hong Kong 'breakers, she arrived there on 12 April 1967. France operated thirteen Liberty ships on wartime Lend/Lease. Post war purchases took the number to 76.

For standard Liberty ship data, see page 32.

40

KOTA INTAN 1944   **Pacific International Lines (Pte.) Ltd.**   *Singapore*

During World War II the U.S. Army maintained a very diverse fleet of service vessels, specific to their needs. This ranged from large troop transports to small tugs and barges. A large building programme was put in place to produce small service ships to support army requirements that were outside of naval operations. This wartime construction for the army followed several different prototypes. All were small cargo ships, but with differing lengths and cargo gear. The type indicator FS was in no way unique to the small steel cargo ships war built for the U.S. Army. It was a general reference to the freight and supply (FS) ships under army control. Many vessels of pre war vintage were operated by the U.S. Army with FS hull numbers. When reference is made to the FS ships, however, it is the small, steel hulled, war built coasters that usually come to mind, craft that were given FS numbers instead of

names. The length of these vessels varied between 114 and 180 feet. Most familiar to this writer are the 180 footers and the slightly smaller 177ft ships, with a lighter mast set midway along the foredeck.

Kota Intan was built by Higgins Industries, New Orleans and delivered to the U.S. Army as **FS-189**. Sold to Mollers Ltd., Hong Kong and renamed **Edith Moller** in 1947, she was later seized by Chinese Nationalist forces and used for raids against the mainland. From 1951 she traded as the **Angelina** for Sun Cheong S.N.Co., Hong Kong, becoming the **Kota Intan**, after sale to P.I.L., Singapore, in 1967. Sold in 1977, the ship was renamed **Lee Wah** by Panamanian owners.

Length	180' 00"	Gross tons	564
Beam	32' 00"	Engines	2 x oil 4SA
Draught	12' 05"		

LANE VICTORY   A Photo Essay

The **Lane Victory** has been preserved. A working monument to her class, American design and wartime shipbuilding. It was back in the late 1980s that two World War II Merchant Marine veterans began turning their dream into reality. Joe Vernick and John Smith, joined by many other veterans, seamen, supporters and friends, formed a group known as the U.S. Merchant Marine Veterans of World War II (USMMVWWII). Based in Los Angeles, the group made wheels turn very quickly. Ideas soon became projects. Washington was canvassed on the issue of veteran status for former WWII merchant seamen. The setting up of a newspaper and information projects publicised the group and merchant marine history. The public and the maritime industry were invited to support the biggest project of all . . . to preserve a Victory Ship. It is indeed fortunate that Captain Walter Jaffee was the Superintendent of the Suisun Bay Reserve Fleet. His feeling for the ships in his care, and vision for the future, were well matched to the goals of the USMMVWWII.

During her reserve fleet years **Lane Victory** was always a show ship. She had been maintained to a standard that would demonstrate to official visitors the ongoing value and potential of the reserve ships. What the fleet could be in a time of national need. This silent duty that she had carried out for almost 20 years made her ideal for the preservation project that was gathering support.

Many problems were encountered. Bureaucratic, financial and logistical, they were all overcome. On 7 June 1989 the USMMVWWII were given title to the **Lane Victory** by way of a Deed of Gift from the U.S. Government. As with the Liberty ships **Jeremiah O'Brien** and **John W. Brown**, this had been achieved by a small group who recognised no limits in the drive to reach their goal. As a training exercise, the U.S. Navy tug **Narraganset** towed the **Lane Victory** to Los Angeles in June 1989. Since that date preservation has been an ongoing success. Regular public cruises and open days are held.

Left   The bridge and foredeck, May 1989. Down below Victory ship spare parts have been stowed and made secure. Granted official permission, and assisted by the U.S. Navy, volunteers worked hard to load the **Lane** with an assortment of deck and machinery equipment, before her tow voyage began.

Above   A door is closed, a new door opens. The **Lane Victory** at Suisun Bay, May 1989. Just days before her move to Los Angeles, the port of her birth, her home for the future.

Right   The wheelhouse May 1989. All the trappings of the voyages to Vietnam remain. Tide tables, charts and navigational notes. Customs forms, both American and Vietnamese, interspersed with crew lists. Posters warn of the danger from riverbank snipers when sailing on the Mekong. Silent testimony to the most recent service the nation had received from the Victory ships of World War II.

Above   The **Lane Victory** has featured in several movies and TV films. December 1994 saw her briefly renamed **Tae Kuk Seattle** for one of her screen roles.

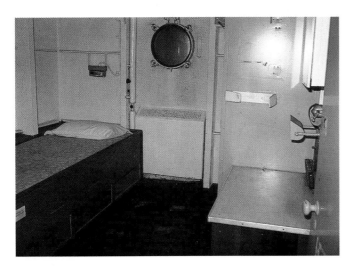

The **Lane Victory** was delivered in June 1945 by the California Shipbuilding Corporation, Los Angeles. On 2 July 1945, with a crew of 58, plus 12 armed guards, she departed Los Angeles loaded with war supplies to support the final weeks of the Pacific War. This was the start of eight voyages, covering ports in Europe, the Mediterranean, the Middle East and Asia. The year 1950, and the Korean conflict, ended two years in the reserve fleet. Extensive service in Korean waters and further visits to Europe followed, before going back into reserve in 1953. January 1967 saw her again heading west across the Pacific, this time to Vietnam. The **Lane Victory** ended her Vietnam service in April 1970 and returned to Suisun Bay.

For standard Victory ship data, see page 47.

Left   An officer's cabin.

JEFFERSON CITY VICTORY 1945   Victory Carriers Inc.   *New York*

Jefferson City Victory on the Canadian Great Lakes, 1960. The contrast provided by backlighting in this photo seems to emphasise the distinctive Victory Ship silhouette. Derricks are topped off for a coastal passage, prop partly out of the water and a stiff breeze playing with the Stars and Stripes. The funnel colours belong to Victory Carriers Inc. of New York. Part of the Onassis group, the company was founded in 1949. They operated a number of Victory ships and T2 tankers. The Oregon Shipbuilding Corporation, Portland, Oregon completed the *Jefferson City Victory* in March 1945. Without change of name, she went to Taiwanese 'breakers in 1973.

There were three basic variations within the overall Victory Ship design. First, came the 272 ships of the VC2-S-AP2 type. These were followed by 141 that were designated VC2-S-AP3. The difference in the two groups was confined to engine power. The AP2s were built with

steam turbines that developed 6,000hp. This was based on the power plant of the C2 design. The more powerful, 8,500hp output of the C3 ships was installed in the AP3 Victories. VC2-S-AP5 was the designator for the Victory hulls completed as Attack Transports for the U.S. Navy. Post war, Victory ships were converted for a number of special duties. Fitted with advanced electronic equipment, they played a significant role in N.A.S.A. space programmes. On 11 August 1960, at the end of the Discoverer XIII mission, the *Haiti Victory* made the first recovery of a man made object from outer space. U.S.N.S. *Private John R. Towle* ex *Appleton Victory* and U.S.N.S. *Private Joseph F. Merrell* ex *Grange Victory* were used in the 1960s as supply ships to Operation Deepfreeze in the Antarctic.

For standard Victory ship data, see page 47.

PERMANENTE SILVERBOW 1944   Permanente SS Corp.   *Oakland*

The bulk cement carrier **Permanente Silverbow** transits San Francisco Bay in this photograph from August 1967. A product of the Oregon Shipbuilding Corporation, Portland, Oregon, completed in June 1944 as the **Silverbow Victory**, her career in bulk cement started early. Permanente Cement Co., Oakland, California purchased her from the U.S. Maritime Commission in 1947. Later in the same year, renamed **Permanente Silverbow** and refitted as a bulk cement carrier by Kaiser & Co., Portland, Oregon, she returned to commercial service. This continued until 1972, when sale to F. Laeisz, Hamburg, West Germany resulted in a change of name and flag. As the **Florida Silverbow**, registered in Panama, cargoes of cement continued to provide her with employment. Sold for scrap to U.S. 'breakers, Ferromar Inc., she was broken up at Brownsville, Texas in 1985.

Permanente Silverbow, as well as the company that converted her for the bulk cement trade, were all part of the huge industrial empire controlled by Henry J. Kaiser. Born in 1882, Henry J. became a civil engineer. From 1914 to 1929 he directed a highway construction company. This led to the building of the Boulder, Bonneville and Grand Coulee Dams. Then came 1940. Europe was engulfed in war. Robert Thompson and his British team went to America, looking for ships. Their needs sat well with Henry J. He had no shipbuilding experience but quickly grasped the situation of emergency and commercial opportunity. As President of Todd-California Shipbuilding Corp. he was a driving force in the setting up of U.S. wartime shipbuilding programmes. Riverbanks were cleared, swamps were drained. New shipyards were quickly built across the U.S.A. So began the biggest shipbuilding programme the world has ever seen. It was indeed a "Bridge of Ships".

For standard Victory ship data, see page 47.

CLEOPATRA 1944

United Arab Maritime Co.

Cairo, Egypt

With the Liberty Ship programme in place, U.S. Maritime Commission planners looked ahead . There was need for ships that were larger, faster and able to sail without the protection of convoy. Ships that would be suited to the liner trades in a post war world. The result was the Victory Ship, an all-American design, in the same concept as the British "Empire Standard Fast" type (see **Benhiant** page 12). Working drawings were completed by the Bethlehem Steel Corporation at Quincy, Massachusetts.Yards were switched from the production of Liberties to the new design. Oregon Shipbuilding Corporation, Portland, Oregon delivered the **United Victory**, the first Victory Ship, on 28 February 1944. Renfrew Navigation Co. Ltd., London, part of the Furness Withy Group, purchased two Victory ships in 1946. It was not until the following year, however, that the **United Victory** was renamed **Khedive Ismail**. **Atchison Victory** became the **Mohamed Ali El Kebir** at the same time.

In 1948 ownership passed to the Khedivial Mail Line, with Egyptian registration. Both ships were converted to accommodate 100 first class passengers. This was for a new passenger/cargo service from Egypt to the U.S. east coast. **Khedive Ismail** ex **United Victory** was renamed **Cleopatra** in 1956. Ownership passed to the Egyptian Government, in the form of the United Arab Maritime Co., in 1960. After leaving Hartlepool on 13 November 1975 a boiler explosion injured several crew members, one fatally. Pakistani shipbreakers ended the ship's days at Gadani Beach in 1981. This 1963 view shows an aesthetically pleasing passenger conversion. The rebuilt bridgefront and extended accommodation sit well with the original cargo gear.

Length	455' 02"	Gross tons	8,193
Beam	62' 01"		(original 7,612)
Draught	28' 07"	Engines	2 x steam turbines

HONGKONG GRACE 1944

C. Y. Tung

Hong Kong

As the **Waco Victory**, the **Hongkong Grace** was delivered by the California Shipbuilding Corporation, Los Angeles in August 1944. Belgian owners Compagnie Maritime Belge (CMB) purchased her from the U.S. War Shipping Administration in 1947, giving her the name **Vinkt**. CMB operated several Victories in their fleet. Others included **Burckel**, **Steenstraete** and **Marchovelette**. **Vinkt** served the company well until 1965, when sold to Hong Kong owner, C. Y. Tung. Renamed **Hongkong Grace**, she hoisted the Liberian flag. The shipping empire controlled by C. Y. Tung was vast. Its ships, with their yellow funnels and stylised red and white cherry blossom logo, traded worldwide. In the early 1970s Tung's Orient Overseas Line maintained an around the world passenger service with the **Oriental Carnival**, **Oriental Esmeralda**

and **Oriental Rio**. These were formerly the ships of the New Zealand Shipping Co.'s **Rangitane** class. C. Y. Tung purchased the liner **Queen Elizabeth** from Cunard in 1970. As the **Seawise University** she was destroyed by fire at Hong Kong in 1972.

This view shows the **Hongkong Grace** limping into Cape Town on 18 May 1973. Two days earlier she had been in collision with the 1956 built, 33,253 dwt tanker **Mina** off Mossel Bay. After temporary repairs she resumed her voyage to New York. In 1973 owners would certainly not entertain large repair accounts for World War II standard ships. **Hongkong Grace** was sold to Taiwanese breakers and arrived at Kaohsiung on 7 December 1974.

For standard Victory ship data, see page 47.

MORMACPINE 1945

Moore-McCormack Lines

New York

In the Pacific War Allied forces had "island hopped" from Guadalcanal to Iwo Jima and Okinawa. From these forward bases the Japanese home islands were within range of the new B-29 bombers. Huge forward supply depots were being set up. The stage was set for the invasion of Japan. It was 1945. The Oregon Shipbuilding Corporation's yard at Portland completed the **Brown Victory** in March that year. She departed Seattle loaded with a cargo of military supplies and arrived off Okinawa on 19 May. This maiden voyage took her well within the war zone. In July, while off the island of I-Shima, the **Brown Victory** was hit by a Japanese Kamikaze suicide bomber. There was extensive damage. A U.S. Navy tug helped her to reach Saipan where her cargo was discharged and temporary repairs made.

Lessons learnt from the building of the Liberty ships ensured that the Victory design did not suffer from the same degree of hull plate fracture.

Some Victory ships did develop cracks in bulwark capping rails and braces. **Brown Victory** was one of five Victories found to have developed fractures in a mast. Although the fracture was near a welded area, the impact from the Kamikaze attack could well have contributed.

In 1947 **Brown Victory** became the **Mormacpine**, under the house flag of Moore-McCormack Lines. She sailed on the company's services to South America and Europe for the next 23 years. Sale to Taiwanese 'breakers was finalised early in 1970. Her last homeward voyage for Moore-McCormack started at Montevideo on 7 April. The following month she loaded a military cargo, on Government account. Exactly as she had done back in 1945, the **Mormacpine** headed across the Pacific with supplies for the U.S. armed forces. She then sailed from Saigon on 15 July 1970 bound for the 'breakers at Kaohsiung.

For standard Victory ship data, see page 47.

HOPE VICTORY 1945   U.S. Department of Commerce   U.S.A.

The Vietnam War was the swansong of the Victory Ship. As the conflict escalated, so too did the need for support services. Large numbers of Victories were available from the U.S. Reserve Fleets. At South East Asian ports, a large percentage of cargo handling was carried out in anchorages, with the use of the ship's gear and barges. Along with other World War II standard types, the Victory ships were ideal for the task at hand.

During the Vietnam years, as in World War II, the management of government owned merchant ships was put in the hands of established shipping companies. The operator was responsible for the running of the ship and its crewing. The government provided the cargo. **Hope Victory** was one of eight Victory ships assigned to Matson Lines during the years of the Vietnam War. Six ships remained painted overall grey. Only two, **Xavier Victory** and **Hope Victory**, were given the buff funnel and blue "M" of Matson Lines. Numerous engine breakdowns caused

the ships to divert to Honolulu for repairs. This reflected on the proud reputation of the Company. It was publicity that Matson did not want. The funnels were repainted grey! For the **Hope Victory** the swansong ended on arrival at San Francisco, 21 July 1969. She was returned to the reserve fleet. Indian 'breakers purchased her for US$396,000. She made her final voyage under tow, arriving at Alang, India on 10 May 1990. The Permanente Metals Corporation, Yard No.2, at Richmond, California, delivered her in May 1945. For 45 years she retained the same name, carried U.S. Government cargoes and spent most of her life in reserve.

This view of the **Hope Victory** shows her berthed at San Francisco. Directly from the Suisun Bay Reserve Fleet, her Vietnam years were about to begin.

For standard Victory ship data, see page 47.

FLYING SPRAY 1944

American Export Lines

New York

From 1963, comes this view of the *Flying Spray*. The sideport doors, as fitted to some C-1s, can be seen along the side of the hull. As the *Cape Nome*, she came from the yard of Pusey & Jones Corporation, Wilmington, Delaware in August 1944. Although sold to Savannah Line, New York in 1947 she continued to trade under her original name. As the *Flying Spray*, she was a part of the American Export Lines fleet from 1951 until 1968. The Panamanian flag replaced the Stars and Stripes in 1968, after sale to Sun Fast Maritime Co. Inc. This company was actually owned by James Patrick & Co. Proprietary Ltd., Sydney, Australia. Named *Tia Pepita*, she tramped worldwide, until being scrapped at Hong Kong in 1970.

Ships of the C1 type were very popular with Norwegian owners. A total of 27 sailed under the Norwegian flag in the post war years. *La Estancia*, owned by Buries, Markes & Co., London was the only C1 to

see commercial service with a United Kingdom owner. *Wairimu* ex *Cape Alva* and *Wairata* ex *Cape Igvak*, as part of the Union Steamship Company fleet, maintained a service from New Zealand to Singapore and India for almost 20 years. The *Cape St. Vincent* was sold to Egypt in 1947. Rebuilt with passenger accommodation, she served as a transport (and perhaps a pilgrim ship) until being sold to Egyptian 'breakers in 1980.

	C1-A (shelter deck)	C1-B (full scantling)
Length	412' 03"	412' 03"
Beam	60' 00"	60' 00"
Draught	23' 06"	27' 06"
Gross tons	5,028	6,750
Engines	2 x steam turbines or 2 x oil 6cy	

CAPE MARTIN 1944   **U.S. Department of Commerce**   *U.S.A.*

The smallest of the original U.S. Maritime Commission designs, the C1s were produced in two basic types, the C1-A and the C1-B. Although generally the same, there were important differences in the two variations. C1-As were shelter deck ships while the C1-B was of the full scantling design. The bulkheads separating the cargo holds only went to the second deck in the A-type. They were watertight to the weather deck in the B-type. The C1-B was of stronger construction. Both steam and motor ships were produced within each type. On the C1-A the side plating of the accommodation was recessed just forward of the lifeboat, thus forming a small boat deck. The side superstructure plating was flush with the hull on the C1-B, the lifeboats being set on top of the accommodation, level with the bridge. For details see *Flying Spray* (page 51).

The first of the type completed was the *Joseph Lykes*. A C1-B, she was built by the Federal SB & DD Co., Kearny, New Jersey in November 1940. By the end of the war 173 ships of the C1 design had been delivered. In 1943, three C1 hulls were completed for the U.S. Navy as the hospital ships *Comfort*, *Hope* and *Mercy*. A group of thirteen, completed as infantry landing ships, were Lend/Leased to Britain. Renamed with an *Empire* prefix, they were available for the Normandy landings.

The *Cape Martin* was built in 1944 at Wilmington, California by the Consolidated Steel Corporation. In 1974 she was sold to Nicolai Joffe Corporation, Beverly Hills, California for scrap. We see her here at Richmond, California in April 1975, awaiting the shipbreakers.

FLYING INDEPENDENT 1944   **American Export Lines**   *New York*

This view of the **Flying Independent** was taken at noon, 25 May 1963 at Port Weller, Ontario, Canada. When viewed with the C1-A, **Flying Spray**, on page 51, the differences between the two variations in the basic C-1 design are clearly seen. As the **Cape Domingo**, **Flying Independent** was a product of the Consolidated Steel Corporation, at Wilmington, California. Sold to American Export lines, she was renamed in 1947. Sperling Steamship & Trading Corporation, New York purchased her in 1966. Still under the U.S. flag, she became the **Harbor Hills**. In contrast to many of her sisters, the ship did not spend idle years in the reserve fleets. She departed Gulfport, Mississippi in June 1968 bound for Taiwanese shipbreakers. By way of Visakhapatnam, India, the **Harbor Hills** arrived at Kaohsiung on 23 August.

On 28 December 1951 the C1-B, **Flying Enterprise** ex **Cape Kumukaki** owned by Isbrandtsen Co., Inc., New York, featured in casualty reports. On passage from Hamburg to New York she encountered a severe storm. A crack developed across the deck and down the sides of the hull. The ship developed a 60 degree list to port and the engine stopped. For thirteen days, the world watched the drama unfold off the south coast of England. The crew was plucked to safety in extreme conditions, but Captain Henrik Carlsen refused to leave his ship while there was a chance she might be saved. The British tug **Turmoil** arrived and her Chief Officer, Kenneth Dancy, risked his life to board the slowly sinking ship to help secure a tow line. Dramatic photographs accompanied the headlines. The two men were forced to jump for their lives as the ship lay on her beam ends, awash in the heavy seas. At 1612 on 10 January 1951 the **Flying Enterprise** sank. This epic salvage attempt, the devotion to duty of the men involved and the name **Flying Enterprise** will long be remembered.

PUTUMAYO 1945

Corporacion Peruana De Vapores

Callao, Peru

It was the nature of the Pacific War that dictated the requirement and specifications which led to the building of 239 C1-M ships. After the Battle of Midway the expansion of Japan's Pacific Empire was halted, then slowly reversed. The island chains of the western Pacific were rungs of a ladder that would lead to Japan's doorstep. Guam, Saipan, Ulithi, Iwo Jima and Okinawa were just some of those island rungs. Each new toehold increased the problem of supply and logistical support. There was a need for a large number of small cargo ships, built to match the requirements. In August 1944 the first C1-M was delivered. The average crew was around 35. Most C1-Ms were named after maritime ropework, knots and hitches e.g. **Long Splice** and **Clove Hitch**. Others were given the prefix **Coastal**. Some were Lend/Leased to Britain and carried names prefixed **Hickory**.

One of eleven of the C1-M type ships built by Globe Shipbuilding

Co., Superior, Wisconsin, **Putumayo** was launched as the U.S. Navy cargo ship **Pipestone** (AK 203). This was not to be, and she was completed in April 1945 as the **Coastal Explorer**. Corporacion Peruana De Vapores of Callao, an operator controlled by the Peruvian Government, purchased her in 1947. **Putumayo** served the company for 21 years, mainly in the coastal trades from the U.S. to South American ports. Peruvian ownership continued after her sale, in 1968, to Naviera Panamar S.A., also of Callao. Renamed **Felipe**, she was registered in the ownership of Gold Shipping S.A., Panama until sold to Spanish shipbreakers in 1974. This 1964 view shows a C1-M-AV1 in its original configuration.

Length	338' 08"	Gross tons	3,805
Beam	50' 03"	Engines	Oil 2SA 6cy
Draught	23' 04"		

PAUL H. TOWNSEND 1945   **National Gypsum Co.**   *Wilmington, California*

This 1960 photo shows a rather dramatic conversion, from C1-M cargo ship, to bulk cement carrier. All the masting and cargo handling gear have been removed and the hull lengthened by 94 feet. The forecastle, slightly lengthened, supports a bridge in the style of the Canadian and U.S. Great Lakes bulk carriers. The original bridge and superstructure aft has been transformed into crew accommodation. Compare this rebuilding aft, with the original styling of the **Putumayo**, on the previous page. It would seem that the kingposts, bridge and monkey island have simply been removed, leaving the remains of the original, to create the "new" superstructure.

The **Coastal Delegate** was completed by the Consolidated Steel Corporation, Wilmington, California in September 1945, after having been launched as the **Hickory Coll**. Sold in 1947 to Agwilines Inc., New York, she worked in the general cargo trades, retaining the name

Coastal Delegate until 1952. In that year conversion to a bulk cement carrier was carried out by Bethlehem Steel Co., Hoboken, New Jersey and she was renamed **Paul H. Townsend**. After the demise of Agwilines, ownership passed to the Huron Portland Cement Division of the National Gypsum Co. The lengthening of the hull followed later, in 1958. As of 1995, she remains on the Great Lakes, and continues to carry the name **Paul H. Townsend**.

The C1-M type has been subjected to many conversions over the years. They have served as drilling ships, dredgers, heavy lift vessels, gas tankers, research and missile tracking ships for the U.S. military as well as providing transport and accommodation for religious groups.

Length	431' 09"	Gross tons	4,302
Beam	50' 01"	Engines	Oil 2SA 6cy
Draught	21' 07"		

HELLENIC SAILOR 1939   **P. G. Callimanopulos**   *Piraeus, Greece*

In 1937 the United States Maritime Commission released plans and specifications that led to the construction of the C2 type. Key features of the design were the requirements for speed and standardisation. The possible naval use of the ships demanded a service speed in excess of 15 knots, well above the average for cargo ships in 1937. Contracts were first given to the Tampa Shipbuilding & Engineering Co. in Florida and the Federal Shipbuilding & Drydock Co., Kearny, New Jersey. The **Challenge**, completed by the Federal SB & DD Co. in July 1939 was the first C2 delivered.

The **Hellenic Sailor** was built by the Sun SB & DD Co., Chester, Pa. and completed as the **Mormacwren**, in August 1939. Her service with Moore-McCormack Lines ended in 1941, when she was taken over by the U.S. Navy. As the U.S.S. **Algorab** (AK 25), she supported the Allied landings at Port Lyautey, Morocco in November 1942. Arrival at Noumea,

New Caledonia in January 1943 heralded her move to the Pacific theatre of operations. She remained with the Fleet, supporting the U.S. advance up to Okinawa, returning to the U.S. in May 1945. Sold in 1947, she was renamed **Kamran**, registered in Panama with ownership reported as being in the hands of Wallem & Co., Hong Kong. The following year, sale to Cie. Maritime Belge took her to the Belgian register and she became the **Mongala**. P.G. Callimanopulos owned and operated her, as the **Hellenic Sailor**, from 1954 until June 1973. Renamed **Aloha** (originally reported as **Aloian**), she departed Piraeus on 8 August 1973 for a final voyage that ended in the shipbreaking yards of Kaohsiung on 23 December 1973. She is seen here at Cape Town on 25 September 1972.

Length	459' 00"	Gross tons	6,281
Beam	63' 02"	Engines	Oil 2SA 4cy
Draught	27' 09"		

FLYING GULL 1941   **American Export-Isbrandtsen Lines Inc.**   *New York*

In 1941 the Robin Line of New York took delivery of six powerful, 15 knot cargo ships for their services to Southern Africa. Of modified C2 design, all were built by the Bethlehem Steel Co., Sparrows Point, Maryland. The gathering war clouds of 1941 soon engulfed the U.S.A. and the new Robin Line ships were diverted to national service. The second of the six ships was completed as the **Robin Doncaster** in April 1941. Almost immediately she was taken on charter by the British Government. At this time the Ministry of War Transport operated several U.S. flag ships, helping to support the large movement of British and Commonwealth troops to the Middle East. After being returned to the U.S.A. during 1942 she resumed Robin Line services. In October 1943 the **Robin Doncaster** was delivered for conversion to a troopship, to be operated by the U.S. Army, but as a "Navy allocation". She emerged on 4 January 1944 with accommodation for 1,756 troops. The **Robin**

Doncaster arrived at Seattle on New Year's Day 1946, ending almost five years of war service. After a short stay in the Reserve Fleet at Lee Hall, Virginia she was returned to the role of a cargo ship.

Ownership passed to Isbrandtsen Co., Inc, New York in 1957 and the **Robin Doncaster** became **Flying Gull**. Her owners were restyled American Export-Isbrandtsen Lines Inc. in 1962. Her final voyage ended at Baltimore on 7 April 1968. Sold to U.S. buyers, she was resold, and under tow the ship left Baltimore on 26 May 1968, bound for shipbreakers at Bilbao. This 1963 photo shows the unusual lines of the C2-S type, futuristic for a design with its origins in the late 1930s.

Length	479' 08"	Gross tons	7,085
Beam	66' 06"	Engines	2 x steam
Draught	28' 11"		turbines

HELLENIC DOLPHIN 1944

P. G. Callimanopulos

Piraeus, Greece

An overcast sky blends with the grey hull of the *Hellenic Dolphin* as she departs from Cape Town on 30 August 1972, bound for Mombasa. Less than two years later her career ended at the hands of Spanish shipbreakers. Her builders, Moore DD Co., Oakland, California delivered 71 C2-S-B1s between January 1943 and June 1945. Completed in 1944 as the *Flying Mist*, she was sold in 1946 to Compania Sud Americana De Vapores, Valparaiso, Chile, who renamed her *Imperial*. For nineteen years, apparently without major incident, she served her South American owners. Purchased by Callimanopulos in 1965, she traded mainly from Mediterranean ports to South and East Africa, under the name *Hellenic Dolphin*. This ended with her delivery to the shipbreakers at Gandia in January 1974.

The development of the type can be clearly seen when comparing this view of the *Hellenic Dolphin* with the early, almost prototype C2, *Hellenic Sailor* on page 56. As completed, the later C2-S-B1 ships provided accommodation for eight passengers. The majority were built as shelter deckers, but there was a full scantling modification produced in small numbers. The five holds were served by unusual tapered kingposts, which also acted as vents for the cargo spaces. Lockers were fitted for a limited amount of refrigerated cargo.

Length	459' 06"	Gross tons	7,989
Beam	63' 01"	Engines	2 x steam
Draught	27' 08"		turbines

AFRICAN GROVE 1944   **Farrell Lines Inc.**   *New York*

The Canadian Great Lakes in 1967 is the setting for this portrait of the **African Grove**. Prominent is the unusual bridgefront, with the protruding wheelhouse, also the unusual C2 bow form, with its very fine entry to the water. The stem was vertical from the forefoot, to the area of the 17ft draught mark, from where it developed into a pleasant rake, giving the impression of speed. The hawsepipe was not fitted with a tripping bar as in the Victory ship design. Viewed from the stern, one could be forgiven for thinking that these vessels did not have a raised poop. Solid bulwarks almost concealed the three island type hull construction. The tall funnel of the **African Grove** was a feature of the turbine driven ships. The diesel powered C2s featured a shorter funnel, set well aft on the superstructure. This caused a problem with soot settling on the decks and funnel height was increased.

Gauntlet was completed in 1944 by the Moore DD Co., Oakland, California. Purchased by Farrell Lines in 1947 and renamed **African Grove**, she operated with other C2s on the company services from the U.S.A. to African ports.

For the **African Grove**, her 25 year service with Farrell Lines ended with a sale to U.S. shipbreakers, Lipsett Inc., followed by resale to a Spanish 'breaker. Her final voyage appeared to have been completed, when she arrived at Ferrol under tow on 15 October 1969. This was not quite the end, however, as the old ship was moved to Cadiz and then to Puerto de Santa Maria where, it would seem, she was broken up.

For C2-S-B1 type data, see page 58.

AMERICAN FORESTER 1945   **United States Lines**   *New York*

The expectations of the C2 design, back in 1937, served the ships well in practice. In this view from late 1966 the **American Forester** was still operating a cargo liner service for the prestigious United States Lines. Although over 20 years old, the speed and general layout of the C2s enabled them to sail into the early days of the container era, many without alteration. Full container conversions were given to some C2s.

    American Forester was the last of the C2-S-B1 type built by Moore DD Co., Oakland, California. As the **Carrier Pigeon**, she was delivered in June 1945 to the U.S. War Shipping Administration and registered at San Francisco. Sold to the United States Lines in 1946, she went into their commercial service after being renamed **Pioneer Wave**. The majority of the cargo ships in the fleet were named with the prefix **American**. This was to indicate that the vessels were engaged in the U.S.-Europe trade. Other ships, used on trans-Pacific services, were given names prefixed **Pioneer**. In practice this policy was not strictly adhered to and ships often "cross traded", as company services demanded. As part of this policy, **Pioneer Wave** was renamed **American Forester** in 1957. Arrival at Jacksonville, Florida on 21 December 1969 marked the end of her service with United States Lines and she was laid up. Sale to another American company, Amercargo Shipping Corporation, came quickly, along with a new name, **Amerwood** (see **Amercrest**, page 61). The next voyage was her last and the shipbreakers at Kaohsiung took delivery of her in July 1970.

    The C2 type was popular in the post war years with U.S. flag operators. They also served both the U.S. Navy and the Military Sea Transportation Service (M.S.T.S.) in a wide range of support roles. These included Antarctic voyages to the U.S. base at McMurdo Sound.

For C2-S-B1 type data, see page 58.

AMERCREST 1946

Amercargo Inc.

New York

The C2-S-AJ1 was a full scantling variation of the standard C2 design. This allowed a commercial operator the advantage of being able to alter the tonnage to suit trading conditions. There was accommodation for eight passengers and some provision for refrigerated cargo.

Completed as the **American Traveler**, the **Amercrest** was one of ten C2-S-AJ5 ships. They were a modified version of the C2-S-B1 type and especially suited to the requirements of the U.S. Lines. Built by the North Carolina Shipbuilding Corp., Wilmington, North Carolina and delivered directly to the U.S. Lines in February 1946, she served the company until 1969, when sold to Amercargo Inc. and renamed **Amercrest**.

The **American Pilot** was also a product from Wilmington. A C2-S-AJ1, she was delivered to the War Shipping Administration in September 1945 as the **Onward**. Under two names she served the U.S. Lines for 24 years, firstly as the **Pioneer Gulf** from 1948, and then as the **American**

Pilot. Without further change of name she was also sold to Amercargo Inc. in 1969.

These two ships that had started life from the same shipyard within months of each other, were destined to end their days together in the scrapyards of Kaohsiung. In this photo from Port Molate, San Francisco Bay, February 1972, we see the **Amercrest** and the **American Pilot** being prepared for a trans-Pacific tow to Taiwan. The tug **Arthur Foss** is alongside the **Amercrest** to assist rigging the towing gear. The port anchor has been unshipped and the chains that will support a towing bridle, hang ready. White paint on the stem will serve as the all important draught indicator to the towing crew. Rigged in tandem tow, both ships departed San Francisco on 14 February. By way of Honolulu, they reached Kaohsiung in early April 1972.

Technical data is similar to that for the C2-S-B1, see page 58.

EXPEDITOR 1943

American Export Lines

New York

The vertical stem, absence of rake and a counter stern, seen in this 1962 photo of the *Expeditor*, indicates a design that pre-dates World War II. It was in 1938 that the American Export Lines and U.S. Maritime Commission jointly produced a design that became the first of the C3 contracts. Eight ships were built by the Bethlehem Steel Co., Quincy, Mass., the first being delivered in September 1939. The vessels were operated by American Export Lines on their services from the east coast of the U.S. to Mediterranean ports and carried names prefixed *Ex*.

Between 1943 and 1946 the Bethlehem Steel Co., Sparrows Point, Maryland produced another fifteen ships, almost identical to the earlier buildings. The first of this group, laid down in 1942, was the *Excelsior*. She was taken over by the U.S. Navy during construction and completed in June 1943 as the attack transport U.S.S. *Windsor* (APA 55). Sent to the Pacific, she supported U.S. amphibious landings, starting in January

1944 with the assault on Kwajalein. Later operations included deployments to Bouganville, New Guinea, Saipan, Peleliu, Leyte and Okinawa. During the final months of 1945 the ship was part of the massive "Magic Carpet" operation, returning U.S. service personnel and equipment to the U.S.A. After being awarded five battle stars for her Pacific service, the *Windsor* was delivered to the U.S. Maritime Commission in 1946 and renamed *Paul Revere.* Purchased by American Export Lines during 1949, she became the *Expeditor*, and joined the fleet she had been built for six years earlier. Delivery to shipbreakers at Kaohsiung ended her career in 1972.

| Length | 473' 01" | Gross tons | 6,724 |
| Beam | 66' 05" | Engines | 2 x steam turbines |

BUCKEYE STATE 1943   **States Marine Lines**   *New York*

The **Buckeye State** was one of 58 C3-S-A2 vessels built by Ingallis Shipbuilding Co., Pascagoula, Mississippi. Many were rebuilt to serve as escort carriers and naval auxiliaries. Named **Sea Star (II)**, she was completed on 3 December 1943 as a troopship, with accommodation for 2,108. (An earlier C3, **Mormacstar**, had been laid down in 1941 as the **Sea Star**.) Under the management of Matson Navigation Co., **Sea Star (II)** departed New Orleans on 18 December 1943 for the Panama Canal and war service in the Pacific. Apart from one voyage into the Mediterranean in June 1945 she remained in the area, supporting U.S. assault landings. The ship was returned to the management of the War Shipping Administration at Olympia, Washington on 20 December 1946. Renamed **George Luckenbach**, and owned by Luckenbach Steamship Co., Inc., New York, she returned to the Pacific on commercial service in 1949. U.S. ownership continued when she was

sold in 1959 to States Marine Lines, becoming the **Buckeye State**. Records show that for the next fourteen years she traded mainly from the U.S.A. to Asian and Indian ports. Like so many other World War II standard ships, the final years of her career often took her to Vietnam with military cargo. Sold to shipbreakers, she departed from Bombay on 2 July 1973 bound for Kaohsiung, via Chittagong and Singapore. This stern view from 1964 shows off the sheer line of the C3 design. As a wartime troopship she carried the same cargo gear as seen here. Four lifeboats were fitted on the boat deck, plus a large number of life rafts secured to launching frames along the main deck. A large gun tub was mounted on the forecastle with two smaller tubs carried aft of No.5 hold. Weapons of lighter calibre were mounted above the bridge and on either side of the boat deck aft.

For data on this type, see page 65.

LA SALLE 1943

Waterman Steamship Corporation

New York

The C3-S-A2 was the most numerous variation of the C3 type, a total of 94 being produced. In this view the **La Salle** is seen arriving at Cape Town, just weeks before her delivery to Taiwanese shipbreakers at Kaohsiung in November 1974. She is an example of the way most C3s appeared in post war commercial service. The Western Pipe and Steel Co., San Francisco launched her as the **Sea Carp**, on 23 January 1943. While fitting out she was taken over by the U.S. Navy and completed as the attack transport U.S.S. **Clay** (APA 39). Extensive war service in the Pacific followed. While operating off Leyte, and later Okinawa, she fought off Japanese Kamikaze attacks and was lucky to escape without incurring any damage. The ship was finally returned to the U.S. Maritime Commission in May 1946. Stripped of her armament and military hardware, she was purchased by American President Lines in 1948, becoming the **President Johnson**. On trans-Pacific services to

Asia, the vessel served the company until 1968, when sold to Waterman Steamship Corporation. As the **La Salle** the parameters of her trade pattern expanded to include voyages from the U.S. Gulf ports to Southern Africa, India and the Persian Gulf.

Four of the C3-S-A2 type were completed as escort aircraft carriers and another four served as U.S. Navy submarine tenders. After the war two of the carriers were rebuilt as passenger liners for the immigrant trades, becoming the **Fairsky** (Sitmar Line, Italy) and the **Sydney** (Achille Lauro, Italy). U.S. shipowners who operated the C3-S-A2 type included Matson, Luckenbach, Isbrandtsen and Moore-McCormack.

Length	492' 00"	Gross tons	7,995
Beam	69' 07"	Engines	2 x steam
Draught	29' 05"		turbines

RAKI 1943

Nederland Line

Amsterdam, Holland

Thirty-eight C3-S-A1 ships were built, and all were converted to escort aircraft carriers. Thirty-seven came from the Seattle-Tacoma Shipbuilding Co., Tacoma, Washington and just one from the Ingalls SB Co., Pascagoula, Mississippi. The first, **Steel Architect**, was laid down for the Isthmian SS Co., launched in October 1941 and completed as the U.S.S. **Copahee**. The next five ships were also intended for commercial owners but again completed as naval carriers. The remaining vessels were all laid down and delivered as escort carriers. They served with the U.S. Navy, and also the Royal Navy, under Lend/Lease arrangements. In service these ships were an outstanding success. Operating with hunter-killer groups in the Atlantic their aircraft attacked, damaged and sank a number of U-Boats.

The **Raki** was completed as the escort carrier U.S.S. **Bolinas**. After delivery at Tacoma in July 1943 she spent just eleven days with the U.S. Navy before being Lend/Leased to Britain. As H.M.S.**Begum** the vessel

operated mainly in the Indian Ocean until being returned to the U.S. Navy on 4 January 1946. The **Begum**, later renamed **Raki**, was one of four escort carriers purchased by Nederland Line after the war and rebuilt to cargo ship configuration, as seen in this photograph from 1964. Note the prominent fairlead at the top of the stem. This can be seen on wartime photos of the ships when serving as escort carriers. The **Raki** was sold to C. Y. Tung in 1966 and traded as the **I-Yung** until being purchased by Taiwanese shipbreakers in 1974. Similar C3 escort carrier conversions included **Rhodesia Star** (Blue Star Line), **Benrinnes** (Ben Line), **Bardic** (Shaw Savill Line), **Nabob** (Norddeutscher Lloyd) and **Friesland** (Rotterdam Lloyd).

Length	492′ 00″	Gross tons	8,204
Beam	69′ 07″	Engines	2 x steam
Draught	29′ 05″		turbines

RIO COBRE 1945

Elders & Fyffes

London

Looking very graceful, almost yacht like, the **Rio Cobre** is seen here in the New Waterway, outward bound from Rotterdam on 2 July 1969.

Enemy action inflicted heavy losses on the refrigerated ships of the U.S. Merchant Marine during the war years. As a result, the United Fruit Company were granted permission to contract with the Gulf Shipbuilding Corporation, Chickasaw, Alabama for the building of replacement ships. The design for these new vessels was developed from the pre-war units of the United Fruit Company. They were to be fast ships, capable of 18.5 knots and driven by four steam turbines. Accommodation was available for twelve passengers. The U.S. Maritime Administration designator R2-ST-AU1 was given to the type.

Nine were built, the first, **Fra Berlanga**, was completed in February 1945 and operated by the War Shipping Administration. The fifth ship, **Junior**, was delivered to the United Mail SS Co. in December 1945.

Her ownership passed to United Fruit Company in 1959. Ten years later she was transferred to the company's British subsidiary, Elders & Fyffes, and was renamed **Rio Cobre**, under the Red Ensign. Until her sale to Taiwanese 'breakers in 1975 the vessel maintained regular services between U.K. and Caribbean ports. A second group, also comprising nine ships, designated R1-S-DH1, were built by the Bethlehem Steel Corp., Sparrows Point, Maryland between 1947 and 1948. Although smaller and slower than the earlier ships, the features of their design could again be traced back to the pre-war vessels of the United Fruit Company, "The Great White Fleet".

Length	455' 05"	Gross tons	6,845
Beam	61' 02"	Engines	4 x steam
Draught	27' 01"		turbines

MARINE FIDDLER 1945   **U.S. Maritime Administration**   *U.S.A.*

The distinctive C4 type ships came into being after a long and involved design process. Their evolution had started in 1941 when an engines aft cargo ship was designed for American-Hawaiian Lines. The military application was realised and the design was taken over by the U.S. Maritime Commission and given the designation C4. Apart from general cargo ships, the Commission saw these vessels as troopships and tank transports. There was much dialogue between the Navy, Army and Maritime Commission, leading to substantial alteration of the design, before building contracts were awarded to three shipyards. The Kaiser Shipbuilding Company yards at Richmond, California and Vancouver, Washington delivered 55 C4s, with another 20 coming from the Sun Shipbuilding & Drydock Co., Chester, Pa. The troopships, with accommodation for between 2,500 and 3,500 troops, were named after U.S. Army generals (eg **General W. M. Black**), while most of the cargo ships were given the prefix **Marine** (eg **Marine Tiger**). Six were completed as U.S. Navy hospital ships.

In the post war years the C4s steamed into the container era as first generation vessels for companies such as Sea-Land Service Inc. The design also proved suitable for a number of specialist conversions. These included satellite tracking vessels, working with the U.S.A.A.F., and heavy lift ships for commercial operation. This view, showing the bridge detail of the **Marine Fiddler**, was taken in the James River Reserve Fleet in May 1985. She was one of the two C4 ships fitted with 150 ton heavy lift derricks.

For data on the basic C4-type vessel, see page 69.

VALL MOON 1944

Vall Carriers Ltd.

Monrovia, Liberia

The **Vall Moon** is seen here anchored off Port Klang, Malaysia, on 6 March 1975. After 31 years' service her appearance remains almost original, even to the cowl funnel top. The following year the vessel was sold to shipbreakers at Gadani Beach, Pakistan. The first of the C4 type built by Sun Shipbuilding & Drydock Co., she was completed in January 1944 as the **Marine Raven**. On behalf of the War Shipping Administration, the ship was managed by the United States Lines. Her war service started in New York, and by December 1944 she had completed sixteen trooping voyages to British ports. Throughout 1945 extended trooping service took her to French and Italian ports. In the following months the **Marine Raven** passed through the Suez Canal and made calls at Colombo and Manila before crossing the Pacific to Seattle. She carried German prisoners of war to New York

and made further Atlantic voyages before being released from Army service on 9 May 1946.

After fifteen years in the reserve fleet the **Marine Raven** was sold into commercial operation in 1961. As the **Sophie H.** she traded for just one year before her owner, John Hadges of New York, renamed the ship **Vasso**. Her trading pattern at this time was worldwide, very much following the later months of her trooping days. Ownership passed to Ocean Shipping & Trading Corporation of New York in 1965 when she became the **Transpacific**, and then in 1973 she was sold again and given her final name, **Vall Moon**.

Length	520' 00"	Gross tons	11,805
Beam	71' 08"	Engines	2 x steam
Draught	30' 00"		turbines

KENNEBEC 1941   **U.S. Maritime Administration**   *U.S.A.*

Late in 1937 international treaties that had restricted naval power ceased to exist. Agreements limiting the size and make up of sea power since the end of World War I were swept aside as the world was pushed towards war. In the U.S.A. vast naval expansion was planned, and with it came the immediate need for more supply ships, more tankers. For design concepts the U.S. Navy drew from proven commercial examples. The Socony-Vacuum Oil Company vessels, *Mobilube* and *Mobilfuel*, delivered in 1939, became the protoypes for future naval tanker design. Agreement between the U.S. Navy and Socony-Vacuum resulted in defence features being built into a group of six tankers the company was about to order. These changes allowed for a bigger power plant, giving the new ships a speed of 16 knots and strengthening, to allow for the fitting of armaments.

The first ship, *Corsicana*, was launched on 19 April 1941 by the Bethlehem Steel Co., Sparrows Point, Maryland. In January 1942 she was taken over by the U.S. Navy and renamed *Kennebec*. The vessel served with Allied forces in the Atlantic and Mediterranean until July 1945, when she departed the U.S.A. bound for the Pacific. For the next year she served as a station tanker with the occupation force in Japan. Except for short periods of decommission and Maritime Administration reserve, the vessel served the U.S. Navy until entering the Suisun Bay Reserve Fleet in 1970. Although she spent just a few months in commercial service the *Kennebec* indeed represented a milestone in U.S. World War II merchant shipbuilding. Her design concept contributed to the largest class of all, the T2-SE-A1. The *Kennebec* is seen here at Suisun Bay in November 1981.

Length	501' 04"	Gross tons	9,900
Beam	68' 03"	Engines	2 x steam
Draught	36' 09"		turbines

ESSO SAO PAULO 1944　　　**Panama Transport Co. (Esso)**　　　*Panama*

A wartime documentary film features clips of a T2 tanker on trials and later in convoy. We see her labouring in heavy seas, with a deck cargo of P47 fighter aircraft ... a powerful image of U.S. wartime industry. The T2-SE-A1 tanker was to the oil trade what the Liberty Ship was to dry cargo. No other wartime tanker design was as numerous, so recognised, or so successful. Turbo-electric machinery gave the ships a speed of 15 knots, and 481 vessels of the type were delivered between 1942 and 1945. As with the Liberty ships, the T2 was of welded, prefabricated construction. A record was achieved in June 1945 when Marinship Corp, Sausalito, California built and delivered the **Huntington Hills** in just 33 days. A number of the type served with the U.S. Navy, often with a name prefixed **Mission** e.g. **Mission Santa Ynez**. Former T2 crew members whom this writer has met always spoke well of the ships. Good seakeeping, little vibration and comfortable accommodation made them popular.

The **Whitehorse** was delivered in April 1944 by the Sun Shibuilding & Drydock Co., Chester, Pa. The following month she collided with the U.S. tanker **Pan Maryland** at New York and required bulkhead repairs and two new plates. Purchased by Esso in 1947, she was renamed **Esso Cambridge** and then **Esso Sao Paulo** later in the same year. The vessel was lengthened in the aft well deck in 1954. From 1959 until 1962 she traded as the **Sao Paulo**. The **Esso** prefix was reinstated in 1962 and her career ended with Taiwanese 'breakers in 1967. She is seen here in U.S. waters in 1963.

Length	564' 06"	Gross tons	11,307
	523' 06" (original)		10,448 (original)
Beam	68' 02"	Engines	steam turbine
Draught	30' 02"		connected to
			electric motor

ESSO REGULUS 1945   Esso Transport Co. Inc.   *Panama*

The Maritime Commission T1-M tankers were small vessels, intended for coastal and short sea services. The design was split into several sub types. The first twelve ships, designated T1-M-A1, were delivered in 1943, followed by a series of petrol carriers for the U.S. Navy. The T1-M -BT2 was the largest of the T1-M designs, a total of 20 being constructed in 1945. Six ships were built by J. A. Jones Construction Co., Panama City, Florida. *Tarantella*, delivered in July 1945, was the second of fourteen sister ships produced by Todd-Houston Shipbuilding Corp., Houston, Texas. Almost immediately after delivery she was transferred to Britain under Lend/Lease and managed by The British Tanker Co. Ltd. (BP), and registered in London.

The vessel was renamed *Djirak* in 1947 and the following year sold to the U.S. based Standard-Vacuum Oil Co. Along with several other T1-M tankers her management was placed with Standard Vacuum Tankvaart

Maats N.V., The Hague, Holland and she was renamed *Stanvac Djirak*.

At this time the Dutch Government had substantial commercial interests in Indonesia. These small tankers were ideal for S.E. Asian operations where small ports often denied access to larger vessels. From 1963 through to 1972 she traded as the Panamanian flagged *Regulus*, becoming the *Esso Regulus* in 1972. After running aground in 1976, repairs were considered uneconomic and the vessel was broken up. As Standard-Vacuum Oil Co. was absorbed by the Esso group the ship, in effect, had the same owners for 28 years. The suitability of the T1-M tankers for S.E. Asian service is thus well illustrated. *Esso Regulus* is seen here at Singapore on 8 March 1975.

Length	325' 00"	Gross tons	3,155
Beam	48' 03"	Engines	Oil 2SA 6cy
Draught	18' 00"		

Index